W. Jeff Lee

A Digest of Patriotic History and Civil Government

W. Jeff Lee

A Digest of Patriotic History and Civil Government

ISBN/EAN: 9783337306540

Printed in Europe, USA, Canada, Australia, Japan

Cover: Foto ©ninafisch / pixelio.de

More available books at **www.hansebooks.com**

A DIGEST

OF

Patriotic History

—AND—

Civil Government

BY

W. JEFF LEE
AND
W. B. GWYNN.

LOUISVILLE, KY.,
1889.

PREFACE.

Dear Friends and Students:—

A pleasant task we have had in searching out and setting in order the truths of history and principles of government found in this little volume. We submit it to you, upon its merits, with the fond hope that you will find it not only a pleasant study, but one that will be of great profit to you and serve to endear to you and help you to exult in the triumph of the long tried principles of our own free and happy government. It is not a commentary but a hand-book that we trust will be satisfactory to you on any point connected with the subject that falls within its province. We fear, of course, that it has many short-comings, but we hope you will not be harsh in your criticisms, but that you will appreciate it for what it is rather than what it is not. You will find the topics and ideas easily led and that they follow on in easy relief, so that it will not weary the brain to comprehend them and thus make them *your own*. The different parts are so arranged as to show the status and relevancy of the times and topics of which they treat, and the chapters are of about the proper length for a pleasant recitation. PART THE FIRST treats of General Principles, Patriotic History, etc. PART THE SECOND treats of the Workings of the Government under the Constitution, and PART THE THIRD is devoted entirely to Kentucky, its History and Local Government, which, we trust, you will find exhaustive and satisfactory. We have endeavored to produce a thorough and satisfactory work and not a mere abortive effort to meet the exigencies of the hour. We have been engaged in teaching for many years and hope we have not taught in vain; and now, if, through this medium, we may be able to enlarge our field of usefulness, our hearts shall overflow with gratitude for such an opportunity. So, with a hope that you will master these principles, and thus live a higher, freer and better life, we are

Yours truly,

THE AUTHORS.

Part First.

GERMS OF CIVIL LIBERTY AND FIRST CONSTITUTIONS.

CHAPTER I.

What is Government? The exercising of a controlling influence or power.

What forms of Government may be mentioned? Patriarchal, Theocratic, Monarchical, Aristocratic, Democratic and Republican.

What is a Patriarchal Government? One in which the father governs. Abraham was a patriarch.

What is a Theocratic Government? One ruled directly by the Diety; as the ancient Israelites were.

What is a Monarchical Government? A government ruled by one person.

How many kinds of monarchy are there? Two, absolute and limited.

What is an absolute monarchy? One in which the governing power is unlimited and arbitrary.

What is a limited monarchy? One in which the power of the ruler is limited by a Constitution.

What is an Aristocratic Government? A government by a select few.

What is a Democratic Government? One by the people direct.

What is a Republican Government? One whose laws are made by representatives elected by the people.

Give the three *principal* kinds of government. Absolute Monarchies, Limited Monarchies, and Republics.

Give examples. Russia, Great Britain, United States.

How many kinds of law are there? Military, civil, and parliamentary.

What are military laws? Those by which soldiers are controlled.

What are civil laws? Those by which citizens are controlled.

What are parliamentary laws? Those by which legislative and other organized bodies are controlled.

What is the foundation of all good government? A CONSTITUTION.

CHAPTER II.

What is a constitution? A bulwark of liberty; a fundamental law of the land; the expressed wishes of the people; a document that prescribes what we may or may not do, and what we shall or shall not do.

Which was the first great constitution? The Magna Charta.

When was it granted? In 1215, June 15.

By whom? King John of England to the Barons.

Why did he grant it? Because it was demanded of him.

Why did the people demand it? To break up despotic rule and secure to themselves more liberty.

What germs of liberty and enlightenment had been planted before this? The right of trial by jury and the founding of Oxford College and other institutions of education and enlightenment.*

When did the first English parliament convene? In 1265.

When did the House of Commons meet in a separate chamber? In 1295.

When were the two houses of parliament recognized as having separate and distinct privileges? In 1370.

When was the "Habeas Corpus" act passed? In 1669.

What does it provide? That the body of any person restrained of his liberty may, upon proper application, be brought before a judge and the reason of his confinement stated; the judge will then determine the amount of his bail, or whether he will remand him to prison or set him at liberty.

When was the "Declaration of Rights" drawn up by the people, signed and accepted by William and Mary? 1689.

What does it secure? Annual parliaments, trial by jury, free elections, and the right of petition.

What great Constitution was adopted 100 years after the Bill of Rights? The Constitution of the United States.

Are these rights incorporated into the Constitution of

---

* The things in this book refer only to English-speaking people.

the United States and also the various State Constitutions? They are.

CHAPTER III.

When was America discovered? Friday, October 12, 1492.

How is America divided? Into South and North America.

Where are the United States? In North America.

How were they settled? By emigrants from Europe.

What is a colony? A company of individuals emigrating from one country and settling in another.

What induced people to leave their native land and settle in the wilds of America? Principally a love of liberty.

Why did they not have liberty in Europe? Because of tyrannical and oppressive rulers.

What nation settled most of the United Colonies? The English nation.

How many original Colonies were there? Thirteen.

Were they all under English rule at the time of the Revolution? They were.

Name them in the order of their settlement. Virginia, New York, Massachusetts, New Hampshire, Maryland, Connecticut, Rhode Island, Dalaware, North Carolina, New Jersey, South Carolina, Pennsylvania, Georgia.

How many kinds of Colonial Government were there? Three.

Name them. Charter, Proprietary and Royal.

Define Charter Government. Government according

to the specifications of a written document, granted by the king, called a charter.

Did all charters give the same privileges? No; they varied greatly; some granted but little liberty, while others gave almost perfect liberty.

Define Proprietary Government. A government in which the proprietor appointed a Governor, under whose authority the Legislature convened.

Define Royal or Provincial Government. One in which the royal authority appointed the Governor and council, or upper branch of the Legislature.

How was the lower branch chosen? By the people.

CHAPTER IV.

Virginia.

When was its first charter granted? 1606.

What did it specify? The government was vested in the London council and the local council; both councils were appointed by the king; the people had no voice.

When and where under this charter was the first settlement made? In 1607, at Jamestown.

When was the second charter granted? In 1609.

How did this differ from the first? It placed the authority in a Governor instead of a local council.

When was the third charter obtained? In 1612.

What change was effected by this? It abolished the London council and gave the stockholders power to regulate the affairs of the Colony.

When and where was the first legislative body ever convened in America. At Jamestown in 1619.

Of what did it consist? A Governor, Council and twenty-two deputies or "Burgesses" chosen by the people.

When were their wishes embodied in a written Constitution? In 1621. What can you say of this? It was the first Constitution ever adopted in America.

When was Virginia made a royal province? In 1624.

New York.

When, where and by whom was it settled? In 1613, at New Amsterdam, by the Dutch.

When did it become an English province? It was surrendered to the Duke of York in 1664 and remained a royal province till the Revolution.

Massachusetts.

When, where and by whom was the first settlement made? In 1620, at Plymouth, by the Puritans.

Did they have royal authority? They did not.

How were they governed? By a written compact, drawn up while on board the Mayflower, under which they agreed to enact just and equal laws.

When was the next settlement made? In 1628.

What was it called? Massachusetts Bay Colony.

How was it governed? By a charter.

When was the union of the Colonies of Plymouth, Massachusetts Bay, New Haven and Connecticut formed? In 1643.

What was the title of this union? "The United Colonies of New England."

What was its object? Common protection against the Indians and to resist the encroachments of French and Dutch settlers.

When was the Navigation Act passed? In 1651.

What did it forbid the colonists to do? To trade with any country except England, and it also restricted the trade among the colonies.

When was Massachusetts made a Royal Province? In 1684.

Why? Because of her resistance to the Navigation Act.

New Hampshire.

When and where was the first settlement made? Near Portsmouth, in 1623.

How was it governed? Similar to Massachusetts till 1741, when it was made a distinct Royal Province.

Maryland.

When and where was the first settlement made? In 1634, at St. Marys.

How governed? By charter granted to Lord Baltimore.

Compare this with that granted to Virginia. This gave the people a voice in making the laws.

What celebrated act did they pass in 1649? The "Toleration Act" which secured to all persons the liberty to worship God according to the dictates of their own conscience.

What took place in 1691? Lord Baltimore was entirely deprived of his rights as proprietor and Maryland became a Royal Province.

How long did this continue? Till 1715, when the fourth Lord Baltimore recovered the Government and religious toleration was restored, and it remained under this proprietary government until the Revolution.

Connecticut.

How settled and when? At various places from 1633 to 1636.

What settlements formed the Connecticut Colony proper? Hartford, Wethersfield and Windsor.

What did they do? Adopted a written Constitution in which they agreed to give all freemen the right to vote.

What can you say of this Constitution? *It was the first written Constitution ever framed by the people for the people.*

When did they obtain a royal charter guaranteeing to them the rights of this Constitution? In 1662.

What happened twenty-five years afterward? Andros, Governor of New England, came from Boston to Hartford and demanded this charter.

What did the people do rather than surrender this precious document? They hid it in a hollow tree since famous as the "Charter Oak."

What did they do when Andros was deposed? Brought forth their charter and remained under its Government till the Revolution.

CHAPTER V.

Rhode Island.

When and where settled? In 1636, at Providence Plantation by Roger Williams.

How governed? At first by Massachusetts but after-afterward by charter obtained by Williams in 1647.

What did the people do on obtaining this charter? They met and elected their officers and agreed on a set of laws guaranteeing freedom of faith and worship to all.

What can you say of this guarantee? *It was the first legal declaration of liberty of conscience ever adopted in Europe or America.*

Delaware.

When and where settled? In 1638 at Wilmington by the Swedes.

How governed? The Swedes were overthrown by the Dutch and the territory was included in Penn's purchase.

When did it become a separate Colony? In 1684 Penn appointed it a Deputy Governor and granted it an assembly, and it remained under this Proprietary Government till the Revolution.

North Carolina.

Under what name was the first settlement made in North Carolina? The Albemarle Colony in 1663.

How governed? By proprietors till 1729, when they ceded their right to the crown and it became a royal province.

New Jersey.

When and where settled? In 1664 at Elizabethtown.

How governed? By proprietors till 1702, when it became a royal province and so remained till the Revolution.

South Carolina.

Under what name was the first settlement made? The Carteret Colony in 1670 on Ashley river.

How governed? By proprietors till 1729 when it became a Royal Province.

Pennsylvania.

How settled? First by the Swedes in 1638, near Philadelphia, who were superseded by the English Quakers in 1681.

How governed? By Wm. Penn, the proprietor, and his heirs till the Revolution.

Georgia.

When and where settled? In 1733 at Savannah by Jas. Oglethorpe, who held the land in trust for the English poor.

How long was it held by trustees? Till 1752, when it became a Royal Province.

RECAPITULATION.

What Colonies were under charter government at the time of the Revolution? Massachusetts, Connecticut, and Rhode Island.

What under Royal? New Hampshire, New York, Virginia, New Jersey, North and South Carolina, and Georgia.

What Proprietary? Maryland, Delaware, and Pennsylvania.

CHAPTER VI.

CAUSES OF THE REVOLUTIONARY WAR.

Name some remote causes. Treating the colonists as inferior beings and denying them social privileges; restricting their commerce with other nations and preventing the manufacture of things useful and necessary to their prosperity and independence.

Name some direct causes. Unjust and tyrannical treatment of the colonists; taxation without representation and other odious legislation.*

Name some of the odious Acts? The Sugar Act, passed in 1764; the Stamp Act, passed in 1765; tax levied on tea, glass, etc., in 1767; the Mutiny Act, and others.

What was the Boston Tea Party? A party of men who labored more than a month to have three ship-loads of tea sent back from Boston.

Did they succeed? They did not. What did they then do? They disguised themselves as Indians and went on board the ships and threw the tea overboard.

What did this provoke the English Parliament to do? To pass the Boston Port Bill.

When was it passed? March 25, 1774.

What did it do? Closed the port of Boston to commerce.

What action did the Colonies take from May 13th to 20th, 1774? They held meetings in the principal cities to consider the state of affairs, and recommended the assembling of a Continental Congress.

How many of the Thirteen Colonies appointed delegates to the First Continental Congress? Twelve; all but Georgia.

How many delegates in the First Continental Congress? Fifty-three.

Name some eminent patriots who were members of it. George Washington, Peyton Randolph, John Adams,

* See Declaration of Independence.

John Jay, Richard Henry Lee, Patrick Henry, Roger Sherman and Samuel Adams.

Who was chosen President? Peyton Randolph, of Virginia.

When and where did it assemble? In Philadelphia, September 5, 1774.

What did it do? It drew up a declaration of Colonial rights.

What else did they do? They agreed to accept as the basis of common action for enforcing these rights fourteen articles, known as the American Association.

Of what was this the origin? The American Union, or United States of America.

By what title are these fourteen articles known? The Articles of Confederation and Perpetual Union of the United States of America.

What was the title of the Colonies at this time? United Colonies of America.

CHAPTER VII.

With what battle did the Revolution begin? Battle of Lexington, Massachusetts, April 19, 1776.

How long did the war last? Eight years.

When was the treaty of peace signed? Sept. 3, 1783.

What aim had the First Continental Congress? To secure their rights and a redress of grievances.

Had the idea of a separation or independence been propagated? It had not.

When did the Second Continental Congress meet? May 10, 1775.

What can you say of the delegates to this Congress?
They were the same men that composed the First Congress with a few exceptions and additions.

Were all the Colonies represented in this Congress? They were.

Were they all still resolved to resist British oppression and maintain a constitutional union? They were.

What idea was now favored? The idea of independence or separation.

Who introduced a resolution to have a committee appointed to draft a declaration of Independence? Richard Henry Lee.

When? June 7, 1776.

When was the committee appointed? June 11, 1776.

Name this illustrious committee. Thomas Jefferson, John Adams, Benjamin Franklin, Roger Sherman and Robert R. Livingston.

Who wrote the report or declaration? Thomas Jefferson.

When did this committee report. July 1st.

When was it adopted by a majority? July 2d.

When was it unanimously adopted, signed and proclaimed to the world? July 4, 1776.

When was the title United Colonies of America discarded for that of "United States of America?" September 9, 1776.

When were the Articles of Confederation and perpetual Union of the United States agreed to in Congress and sent to the States for their approval? November 15, 1777.

When had eight of the State legislatures ratified these articles? July 9, 1778.

When did the last State ratify them? March 1, 1781.

When did the Continental Congress first meet under these articles? March 2, 1781.

What with propriety may the Articles of Confederation be called? The First Constitution of the United States.

How long was the Government carried on under them? Eight years.

CHAPTER VIII.

What was the nature and power of the Articles of Confederation? They were little more than a league of friendship; were very imperfect and fell far short of the present Constitution in authority and power.

Point out some of the great defects in them. There was but one branch of the Government, a Congress, and that had to make the laws and provide for their execution and adjudication, as there was no provision for Executive or Judicial departments.

Give another defect? There was too much power reserved to the States and not enough given to Congress.

What of taxes? Congress could apportion taxes but had no power to levy and collect them, and therefore could not meet the expenses and maintain the credit of the Government.

Give Article Second. "Each State retains its sovereignty, freedom and independence and every power, jurisdiction and right which is not by this Confederation expressly delegated to the United States in Congress assembled."

Were there not also many good points in these articles? There were, and they were afterward incorporated into our present Constitution.

How often did Congress meet? On the first Monday in November every year.

How were its delegates elected? By the State Legislatures, annually.

What rights did the States reserve over their delegates? The right to recall any and all of them at any time and to send others in their stead.

How were they paid? By the States.

How many delegates could each State send? Not less than two nor more than seven.

In determining questions in Congress how many votes did each State have? But one.

How were questions of boundary, jurisdiction, etc., arising between States adjudicated? By commissioners or judges.

How were these appointed. By the parties themselves under the authority of Congre

Should the parties fail to appoint them how wei they chosen? Then Congress chose them by lot.

Was Congress in session continually? No.

For how long a time could it adjourn? Not longer than six months.

How was business transacted when Congress was not in session? By a Committee of the States.

Of what did it consist? Of one member from each State.

What were their powers? Such as Congress conferred on them from time to time.

CHAPTER IX.

What was appallingly manifest at this time to all the great statesmen and patriots? That the present confused state of the Government would soon cause them to lose all that they had gained, and that a new order of things must be instituted and a better government adopted.

What was proposed? A revision of the Articles of Confederation.

What did the present Constitution grow out of? Out of the revision of the Articles.

When, and who took the first steps to revise these Articles? In 1786 the Legislature of Virginia proposed a convention of Commissioners to improve the condition of trade and commerce.

What did these commissioners do when they met? They recommended Congress to call a general convention to revise the Articles of Confederation.

When did Congress call a general convention? In February, 1787.

Where and when did this convention assemble? In Philadelphia, May, 1787.

What convention was this? The one that framed and adopted the present Constitution.

How many States were represented in this convention? Twelve; all except Rhode Island.

What was the character of the members of this convention? They were men of great wisdom, firmness, strong attachment to liberty, and tried patriotism.

Name some of the most prominent? George Washington, Alexander Hamilton, Benj. Franklin, Jas. Madison, and Robt. Morris.

Who was chosen President of the Convention? George Washington.

Who noted down the proceedings of the convention in Short-hand? James Madison.

What are these notes called? The Madison papers.

How many books did they compose? Three large volumes.

How long before they were printed? Fifty years.

How long did this convention hold? Four months and three days.

How were their sessions held? In secret.

Did they readily agree on the Articles of the Constitution? They did not; most of them are the result of long debates, consultations, and compromise.

When was the Constitution signed by the members of the convention? September 17, 1787.

What was then done with it? It was sent to Congress.

What did Congress do with it? Congress acted upon it and sent it to the various States for ratification.

How did the States ratify it? Some by their legislatures and others by conventions.

What number of States had to ratify it before it became a law? Nine.

Was there much difference of opinion in the State Legislatures and conventions concerning the adoption of it? There was, and the people were often nearly equally divided.

How many States had adopted the Constitution July 26, 1788? Eleven.

What did Congress now do? Prepared to enter into the new order of things ordained by the Constitution.

What provisions did they make? Provisions for the election of electors for President and Vice-President, and such other arrangements as were necessary for the new government to begin operations.

When were the first electors chosen? On the first Wednesday in January, 1789.

When did the electors meet and cast their vote for President and Vice-President? On the first Wednesday in February, 1789.

What day was appointed for the government to go into operation? The first Wednesday in March, 1789, which was the fourth day of the month.

What has the fourth day of March since been called? The first day of our political year.

On what day does a President's or Congressman's term of office begin and expire? On the fourth of March.

Was Washington, the first President, inaugurated on the fourth of March? He was not. Why? Because it was impossible to perfect preliminary arrangements to that effect.

When was he inaugurated? April 30, 1789.

What did he do? He immediately chose his Cabinet and put the machinery of the Government into active operation.

What can you say of the choice of George Washington as President? All eyes turned instinctively towards him. With love and confidence he stood "first in war, first in peace, and first in the hearts of his people."

CHAPTER X.

How does the Constitution of the United States together with its Amendments rank as a national document? Very high; it is considered the best in the world.

Was it perfect at the time of its adoption? It was not, it had many defects.

How have some of these defects been remedied? By Amendments.

How many Amendments have been adopted? Fifteen.

When were the first ten made? In 1791.

To what do they relate? To religious, personal, and State rights.

When was the eleventh made? 1797.

To what does it relate? To the Judiciary or Courts.

When was the twelfth made? 1804, September 25.

To what does it relate? To the electors of President and Vice-President, and requires them to cast a separate ballot for each.

What gave rise to this Amendment? In the election of 1800 Jefferson and Burr each received seventy-three votes, and the Constitution did not decide which should be President and which Vice-President.

When was the thirteenth Amendment made? In 1865.

To what does it relate? To the abolition of slavery.

When was the fourteenth made? 1868.

To what does it relate? To the rights of citizens.

When was the fifteenth made? 1870.

To what does it relate? To suffrage or voting.

What Amendment was proposed during the Fiftieth Congress in 1888? One to elect President and Vice-President by the popular vote.

How are Amendments to the Constitution made? By a two-thirds majority vote in Congress, together with the ratification of three-fourths of the several State Legislatures.

Part Second.

THE UNITED STATES.

In what political division do we live? In the United States.

Give the area. About 3,603,000 square miles.

What is the motto of the United States? *E Pluribus Unum* (Out of Many, One).

Population? About sixty-five millions.

Form of Government? A Republic.

What is the Supreme Law of the land? The Constitution.

How long has the Government been in operation under the Constitution? One hundred years.

What of its prosperity under it? Phenomenal; unsurpassed in the history of nations.

How may we refer to the United States? As the "Cradle of Liberty."

What of the liberty of its citizens? Every citizen is a sovereign and has perfect personal, political, civil, and religious liberty.

What is personal liberty? Liberty to go and come when one pleases, and to reside in any place he chooses.

What is political liberty? The right to a voice in the selection of his rulers.

What is civil liberty? Having all the rights and immunities of a citizen.

What is religious liberty? Freedom to worship God according to the dictates of conscience. No national church is established by law.

How do these liberties compare with those of the citizens of other governments? No other governments give such liberties, except such as are modeled after our government, viz., the South American States, France, Switzerland and a few other European governments.

Who ordained and established our Constitution? The people.

For what purpose? "To form a more perfect union, establish justice, insure domestic tranquility, provide for the common defense, promote the general welfare, and secure the blessings of liberty to them and their posterity."

Give the three branches of our Government? The Legislative or law-making department, the Executive or law-enforcing department, the Judicial or law-discriminating or judging department.

CHAPTER I.

LEGISLATIVE DEPARTMENT.

Where is the legislative power vested? In a Congress.

CIVIL GOVERNMENT.

Of what does it consist? Of a Senate and House of Representatives.

How is the word Congress used? Strictly speaking it refers to both branches, but commonly speaking it refers to the lower branch only.

How is the House of Representatives commonly spoken of? As Congress and its members are called Congressmen.

How are members of the upper house designated? As United States Senators.

How many years constitute a Congress? Two years.

How many sessions in each Congress? Two; a long and a short session.

What was the longest session ever held? The 1st session of the fiftieth Congress, which lasted 321 days.

What is the present Congress (1889). The fifty-first.

SENATE.

Of what is the SENATE composed? Of two members from each State, irrespective of area or populaton. Illustrate: Rhode Island, the smallest State, has two Senators, while Texas, the largest, has but two; also Nevada, with only sixty-five thousand people, has two Senators, while New York, with a population of over five million, has only two.

What is the design of this? To protect the smaller States against the more populous ones.

Who are our Senators from Kentucky 1889? Hons. Jas. B. Beck and Jos. C. S. Blackburn.

Who are our Senators at the present time? Supply names according to time.

What is the elgibility of a Senator? He must be thirty years of age, nine years a citizen of the United States, and must be a voter of the State from which he is chosen.

Can a foreign-born citizen be a Senator? He can. Name one. Jas. B. Beck.

Term of office? Six years.

How often may they be re-elected? As often as the people wish.

Who was in the Senate thirty consecutive years? Thos. H. Benton, of Missouri.

Into how many classes are Senators divided? Three.

Why so divided? To maintain the Senate a perpetual body and to have only one-third new members each Congress.

The terms of office of what part expire each Congress? One-third part.

What part are new members? One-third.

What part are old or held-over members? Two-thirds.

HOUSE OF REPRESENTATIVES.

Of whom is the House of Representatives composed? Of persons elected by the people in the various States in proportion to the population.

Who may vote for a Representative? Any one qualified to vote for a member of the lower branch of the State Legislature.

Term of office of a Representative? Two years.

Eligibility? He must be twenty-five years of age, seven years a citizen of the United States, and a citizen of the State from which he is elected.

CIVIL GOVERNMENT.

May a foreign-born citizen be a Congressman? He may.

How often may a Representative be re-elected? As often as the people wish.

Who is our Representative from this district? ———

How would you address a letter to a Representative? This way: Hon. ——— M. C., Washington, D. C.

How many members in the United States Senate at present (1889)? Seventy-six.

Is this number permanent? It is not.

When does it change? Whenever a new State is admitted.

What is the number in the House of Representatives at present? 325.

Does the number change? It does. When? Whenever a new State is admitted and when a general apportion is made.

How often is an apportionment made? Once every ten years.

Upon what does the number of Representatives from each State depend? Its population.

How is the population obtained? By the census.

CHAPTER II.

How often is the census taken? Once every ten years.

When was the first taken? In 1790.

How are census years known? They end with a naught.

How often has it been taken? Ten times.

When will the next one be taken? In 1890.

According to the Constitution how many Representatives must a State have? At least one.

Under this Constitutional provision what States have but one each? Delaware and Nevada.

How many Representatives is each territory allowed? One. What are his privileges? The same as those from the States, except he has no vote.

When is an apportionment made? Within three years after the census is taken.

How do apportionment years end? In 3.

When was the last apportionment made? In 1883.

When will the next one be made? In 1893.

What is the basis of Representation at the present time? One to every 151,911.

Who determines the number of Representatives? Congress.

In 1880 what was the population of the United States exclusive of the Territories and the District of Columbia? 49,871,340.

How do we obtain the ratio or basis of representation? By dividing 49,371,340 by 325, the number of Representatives at the present. Thus: $49,371,340 \div 325 = 151,911$, the present basis.

How many Congressmen has Kentucky? Eleven.

What Congressional District is this? ———

Of how many counties is it composed? (See table of Congressional Districts.)

Name the counties and give the population of each? (See table Congressional Districts.)

CIVIL GOVERNMENT. 31

What is the population of the district? (See table Congressional Districts.)

CHAPTER III.

How many members were there in the first Congress? Sixty-five.

What was the ratio or basis of representation? One to every 30,000.

On this basis how many Representatives would we have at present? Sixteen hundred.

Would it be practicable to legislate with so large a body? It would not; in fact it would be almost impossible to do so?

The following table exhibits the various apportionments that have been made, together with the number of Representatives and the basis of representation:

				No. Reps.	Basis of Rep.
From	1789	to	1793	65	30,000
"	1793	to	1803	105	33,000
"	1803	to	1813	141	33,000
"	1813	to	1823	181	35,000
"	1823	to	1833	212	40,000
"	1833	to	1843	240	47,700
"	1843	to	1853	223	70,680
"	1853	to	1863	234	93,500
"	1863	to	1873	241	127,941
"	1873	to	1883	292	130,533
"	1883	to	1893	325	151,911

What is the greatest number of Congressmen any State has ever had? From 1830 to 1840 New York had forty.

How many had Kentucky during that period? 13.

When was her number reduced to ten? In 1840.

How long was ten her number? Forty years.

How many members in the United States Senate now (1889)? Seventy-six; two from each State.

How many in the House of Representatives? 325.

How many in both? 401.

How many electors in the electoral college of the United States? 401.

How many electors has Kentucky? Thirteen; one for each Representative and United States Senator.

How are United States Senators elected? By the State Legislatures.

When? The second Tuesday after each Legislature convenes.

How does the Legislature proceed to elect a United States Senator? On the second Tuesday after the Legislature convenes the Senate and House of Representatives each takes a separate vote for United States Senator; the next day (Wednesday) at 12 o'clock the Senate rises and proceeds to the hall of the House of Representatives, and there both bodies in joint session take a *viva voce* vote for United States Senator. If there is an election it is so announced. If not, they proceed from day to day in joint session, taking at least one vote a day until an election is made.

How are vacancies in the United States Senate filled? By election, if the Legislature is in session; if not, then the Governor appoints a man to serve till the Legislature does meet.

How are Congressmen elected? By the people, who vote by ballot.

When? On the first Tuesday after the first Monday in November in the even years.

When do their terms of office begin and expire? On the fourth of March in the odd years.

How are vacancies filled? By special election ordered by the Governor of the State.

What is the salary of United States Senators and Congressmen? They get the same, $5,000 per year, (the Speaker of the House and President of the Senate get $8,000 each), and twenty cents per mile mileage for the entire distance traveled both ways to and from their homes to Washington by the most common route. The Government also allows them $125 for stationery, and they formerly had the "Franking privilege."

What was the Franking privilege? The privilege of sending letters and documents through the mails free of postage.

How may their salaries be changed? By law, but such change shall not affect the members of the Congress that made it.

Can members of Congress hold any other office of profit under the United States? They can not.

When and where does Congress meet? On the first Monday in December of each year in the Capitol building at Washington.

CHAPTER IV.

ORGANIZATION OF THE U. S. SENATE.

Who is President of the United States Senate? The

Vice-President of the United States.

When may he vote? Only in case of a tie.

In case of death, resignation, or removal from office, or when the Vice-President becomes President, what would the Senate do? Proceed to elect a President *pro tempore* from among their number.

Would he have a vote? He would, because he is a Senator.

Who are the other officers elected? Secretary, Sergeant at Arms, Post Master and Door-keeper.

Are they members? They are not.

What are the duties of the Secretary? He is the recording officer and it is his business to keep a journal or record of the proceedings.

What are the duties and business of the Sergeant at Arms? He is a sheriff or police officer, and assists the President in keeping order.

What else does he do? He keeps the accounts of the pay and mileage of the members of Congress, prepares checks and draws and pays the money to them.

What is the business of the Post Master? He superintends a post-office in the Capitol for the convenience of members.

What is the business of the Door-keeper? To admit proper persons and to exclude improper ones; he also has charge of the furniture.

What other officer has the Senate? A Chaplain.

How does he obtain his position? By appointment.

What is his duty? To open the daily sessions with prayer.

How many standing committees has the Senate? From thirty to thirty-five.

How are they chosen? By election.

How is the chairman of each committee elected. By a majority vote.

How are the other committeemen elected? By a plurality vote.

How many standing or parliamentary rules has the Senate? Fifty-two.

How many joint rules of the Senate and House? Twenty-two.

What does the Senate now do? It informs the House that it is ready for business.

CHAPTER V.
ORGANIZATION OF THE HOUSE OF REPRESENTATIVES.

Who organizes the House of Representatives? The Clerk of the last House.

How does he proceed? He calls the House to order and reads a list of the members and has the oath of office administered to them.

How is this done? Usually in classes, the members from each State forming a class.

What is next in order? Nomination and election of a Speaker.

Is there often much contest over these elections? There is; in the election of N. P. Banks in 1856 two months were spent and 133 ballots were taken.

After the Speaker is elected how does the organization proceed? The speaker takes the chair and is the presiding officer thenceforth.

What is necessary to complete the organization? The election of the minor officers, viz., Clerk, Sergeant at Arms, Post Master and Door-keeper.

Are they chosen from among the members? They are not.

What are the duties of these officers? The same as those of the Senate.

Has the House also a chaplain? It has.

Is the office of Speaker a very important and responsible one? It is. Why? Because he appoints the committees and thus has power to shape legislation.

What is the most important committee? Committee on Ways and Means.

Has the Senate such a committee? It has not.

How many standing committees has the House? From forty to forty-five.

How many standing or parliamentary rules has the House? 160.

What does the House do when its organization is complete? It notifies the Senate that it is ready for business, and the two Houses by a joint committee notify the President.

What does the President do when he is thus notified? He sends in his annual message.

What is set forth in the "President's Message?" The condition of the government and its relation to foreign governments. It also contains a fiscal report from the various departments, together with suggestions and recommendations for necessary legislation.

What is done with this message? It is received, analyzed and each part referred to an appropriate standing committee.

CHAPTER VI.

LEGISLATION.

What is a "Bill?" The embodiment of a member's wishes in writing.

How is a bill introduced? By leave or permission. All leaves or permissions are granted on certain days.

What are such days called? Leave days.

When a bill is introduced what is done with it? It is referred to the appropriate standing committee.

What do they do? They pass upon it and report it back to the house in which it originated with their opinion of it.

How many readings must it there have? Three, on three different days.

Is that rule invariable? It is not, but may be suspended by a four-fifths vote and the bill be acted on immediately.

If the bill passes what is then done with it? It is sent to the other house where it goes through a similar process.

If it passes that House where is it then sent? To the President for his approval.

If he approves it what does he do? Signs it.

If not what does he do? He vetoes it.

What do you mean by the President's veto? That he sends it back to the House in which it originated with his objections in writing, which are entered in full on the journal.

What is sometimes done with vetoed bills? They are reconsidered and passed over the President's veto.

What vote is necessary to pass a bill over the President's veto? Two-thirds of each House.

What number is necessary to pass a bill in the first place? Simply a majority.

Bills passed over the President's veto must have what signatures? Those of the President of the Senate and the Speaker of the House.

Bills passed with the President's approval must have what signatures? Those of the President of the United States, the President of the Senate and the Speaker of the House.

If the President fails to return a bill within ten days (Sunday excepted) what becomes of it? It becomes a law, unless Congress shall adjourn in the meantime.

CHAPTER VII.

RELATIVE POWERS AND DUTIES OF THE SENATE AND HOUSE OF REPRESENTATIVES.

What are their relative powers and duties? They are co-ordinate, concurrent and exclusive.

What do you mean by co-ordinate? Having equal power.

What do you mean by concurrent? That both houses take part in the legislation.

What do you mean by exclusive? Things pertaining to one House only and over which the other has no control.

Name the things which are concurrent to both

Houses. The adoption of the twenty-two joint rules and all legislation (except the origination of bills to raise revenue), all resolutions and the final adjournment.

What are laws passed by Congress called? "Acts of Congress."

How is every act headed? By the enacting clause. Give it. "Be it enacted by the Senate and House of Representatives of the United States of America in Congress assembled."

Give some of the principal topics of concurrent legislation. To lay and collect taxes, to borrow money, to coin money, to punish counterfeiting, to establish post-offices, to constitute inferior courts, to declare war, to raise and support armies, to provide and maintain a navy, &c., &c.

EXCLUSIVE POWERS.

What powers and duties are exclusive to the Senate? To judge of its own election returns, to punish and expel its own members, to elect its own officers, except its President, to elect its own committees, to make its own standing rules, to hold executive sessions, to try impeachments, and to elect a Vice-President when the electors fail to do so.

How often has the Senate elected a Vice-President? Once.

When, and whom did they elect? In 1837, R. M. Johnson, of Kentucky.

What are Executive Sessions? Secret sessions, held to confirm appointments made by the President and to ratify treaties.

What vote is necessary to confirm an appointment? A majority.

How many to ratify treaties? Two-thirds.

In trial of impeachment of the President of the United States, who presides? The Chief Justice. Why? Because the Vice-President being an interested party might be tempted to use unjust means to convict the President in order to secure the Presidency for himself.

In trials of impeachment how many votes are necessary to a conviction. Two-thirds.

Give a case of impeachment of a President. Andrew Johnson, but the Senate failed by three votes to obtain the necessary two-thirds.

CHAPTER VIII.

Give the exclusive powers of the House of Representatives. To judge of its own election returns, to punish and expel its members, to elect its own officers, to make its own standing rules, to originate bills for raising revenue, the sole power of impeachment, and the election of a President when the electors fail to do so.

How often has the House of Representatives been called upon to choose a President? Twice.

When? First in 1801, when Jefferson was chosen, and next in 1825, when John Quincy Adams was chosen.

When the House of Representatives elects a President how many votes has each State? One.

How many States form a quorum? Two-thirds of them.

How many necessary to an election? A majority.

CIVIL GOVERNMENT.

How was R. B. Hayes elected in 1877? By a joint "Electoral Commission."

Of whom was it composed? Of five United States Senators, five Representatives and five Judges of the Supreme Court.

How was this commission chosen? By Congress.

If the House of Representatives should fail to make a choice by the 4th of March who would become President? The newly elected Vice-President.

What is impeachment? Preferring charges against an office-holder for official misconduct.

Who prefers these charges? The House of Representatives.

Who tries the officer impeached? The Senate.

Who prosecutes him? A committee appointed by the House.

What of conviction? It shall extend only to his removal from office, and disqualification to hold any office of trust under the Government afterward.

Is he subject to indictment and trial by law for the same offense? He is.

In legislative bodies how is voting done? *Viva voce,* by the ayes and noes or unrecorded vote, or by the yeas and nays or recorded vote.

In each branch of Congress what part is necessary to call the yeas and nays. One-fifth.

In each branch of Congress how many constitute a quorum? A majority.

What may a smaller number do? Adjourn from day to day and compel the attendance of the other members.

By what vote may a member be expelled? A two-thirds vote.

How long may one House adjourn without the consent of the other? Not exceeding three days.

What power over the English Congress or Parliament has the Crown? Power to prorogue or adjourn it at any time.

Has our President any such power? He has not, and can only adjourn Congress when the two Houses fail to agree on a time.

CHAPTER IX.

POWERS OF CONGRESS.

Where are the powers granted to Congress enumerated? In Sec. 8 Art. 1 of the Constitution.

(Here read and study that section carefully).

What are taxes? Monies levied and collected by public officials.

How many kinds of taxes are there? Two; Duties or Tariff and Internal Revenue.

What are duties? Money paid on goods imported or exported.

What is a tariff? A list or scale of duties.

Where are these duties collected? At the custom houses. By whom? By custom house officers, who send it to the United States Treasury.

How much is collected annually from this source? About two hundred and nineteen million dollars.

What is the Internal revenue? Taxes laid on certain articles manufactured and sold in the United States; whisky and tobacco being the principal ones.

Who collects this? Officers called Collectors of Internal Revenue.

How much is collected annually from this source? About a hundred and twenty-four million dollars.

What restriction as regards taxes? They shall be *uniform* throughout the United States.

Can Congress borrow money on the credit of a State? It can not; only on the credit of the *United States*.

With whom and where does Congress have power to regulate commerce? With foreign nations, and the Indian tribes, and among the several States.

How long must a foreign-born citizen reside in the United States before he can be naturalized? Five years.

Give the process of naturalization. After he has resided for at least three years in the United States he may declare, before proper authority, on oath, his intention of becoming a citizen of the United States. After two more years, at least, he may take the oath of allegiance, when he must prove by witnesses that he has resided five years in the United States and one year in the State in which he seeks to be naturalized; that he has borne a good moral character, and that he has been well disposed toward our Government.

Can any State or individual coin money or fix the value thereof? No; this power belongs solely to Congress.

How is counterfeiting punished? By laws made by Congress.

Can a State establish a post-office? It can not; it must be done by Congress.

How has Congress promoted science and arts? By copyrights and patent rights guaranteeing to authors and inventors for a specified time the exclusive right to their writings and inventions.

For how long is a copyright given? Twenty-eight years, and may be renewed for fourteen years.

What does it cost to obtain a copyright? One dollar and two complete copies of the work.

Whom should you address? The Librarian of Congress, Washington, D. C.

For how long is a patent right given? Seventeen years. Cost of obtaining a patent? Thirty-five dollars.

How was the Supreme Court established? By the Constitution.

How are inferior courts established? By Congress.

Who has power to declare war, and grant letters of Marque and Reprisal? Congress.

What are letters of Marque and Reprisal? Letters authorizing private persons to seize the property of another nation.

Who is to raise and support armies? Congress.

For how long shall an appropriation of money for such purpose run? Not longer than two years.

Who provides and maintains a navy? Congress.

Who makes the rules for the government and regulation of the land and naval forces? Congress.

To what do the 15th and 16th clauses of this article refer? To the militia.

Over what District does Congress have exclusive control? The District of Columbia.

Do not the citizens of this District have a vote in their government? They do not.

Who has control over the grounds on which forts, magazines, arsenals, dock-yards, custom houses, etc., are erected? Congress.

How are such grounds purchased? By the consent of the State Legislatures.

What right do the States reserve over them? The right to control or arrest their citizens on them.

POWERS DENIED CONGRESS.

Where are the powers denied Congress enumerated? In Sec. 9 Art. 1.

When may the writ of habeas corpus be suspended? Only in cases of insurrection or invasion when the public safety may require it.

Can Congress pass a bill of attainder or an ex-post facto law? It can not.

What is a bill of attainder? An English term, and means an act which inflicts death for treason without trial.

What is an ex-post facto law? A law making an act a crime which was not so when it was committed.

Can Congress lay a capitation or other direct tax unless it is in proportion to the population? It can not.

How are monies drawn from the treasury? Only in consequence of appropriations made by law.

Can Congress grant any title of nobility? It can not.

Can any one holding any office of profit or trust accept any present from any king, prince or foreign state without the consent of Congress? He can not.

How are amendments to the Constitution proposed?
Either by two-thirds of both Houses of Congress, or by two-thirds of the State Legislatures.

When an amendment is made how is it ratified? By three-fourths of the State Legislatures.

CHAPTER X.
EXECUTIVE DEPARTMENT.—PRESIDENT.

In what is the executive power of the United States vested? In a President.

What is the executive power of Russia called? A Czar; of Great Britain, King or Queen; of Germany, Kaiser or Emperor; of France, President.

What is said of the office of President of the United States? It is one of great dignity, responsibility and power.

What should be the character of the President? He should be a man of great ability, prudence, discrimination and firmness.

Who was the first President? George Washington.

How long since he was elected? One hundred years.

Was he re-elected? He was.

What precedent did he establish at the end of his second term? He refused a third term, and this example set by the "Father of his Country" has ever since been regarded as an unwritten law.

Is there any limit to the number of terms prescribed by the Constitution? There is not.

How many Presidents have been re-elected? Seven.

Name them. Washington, Jefferson, Madison, Monroe, Jackson, Lincoln and Grant.

How many had been Vice-President before they were elected President? Three.

Name them. John Adams, Thomas Jefferson and Martin Van Buren.

How many had been Secretary of State? Six.

Name them. Jefferson, Madison, Monroe, J. Q. Adams, VanBuren and Buchanan.

What Presidents died a natural death during their term of office? W. H. Harrison and Zachary Taylor.

Who were assassinated? Two; Lincoln and Garfield.

What father and son were Presidents? John Adams and John Quincy Adams.

Give an instance of grandfather and grandson. Wm. H. Harrison and Benj. Harrison.

What two ex-Presidents died on the same day, 4th of July, 1826. John Adams and Thos. Jefferson.

What other ex-President also died on the 4th of July? James Monroe, in 1831.

What two great Statesmen and Senators never gained Presidential honors? Henry Clay, of Kentucky, and Daniel Webster, of Massachusetts.

The election of what three Presidents was decided by the House of Representatives? Jefferson, John Quincy Adams and R. B. Hayes.

Give the eligibility of a President. He must be a natural-born citizen, thirty-five years of age and fourteen years a resident of the United States.

What is the President's salary? $50,000 per year, $4,166⅔ per month, $136 per day (Sundays included,) $160 per day (Sundays excluded).

How is this paid? Monthly, out of the treasury.

Has it always been this sum? No; it is subject to change by Congress, and was raised from twenty-five to fifty thousand in 1873.

What is the probable total expense of the President for a term, including his salary, clerk hire, waiters, furnishing the White House, &c.? $500,000.

How does this compare with the salaries of the executive heads of European Governments? It is very small; many of the petty sovereigns receive a sum far in excess of this amount.

What is a President's term of office? Four years.

In case of death, resignation, removal or incapability of the President, who would become President? The Vice-President.

CHAPTER XI.

THE VICE-PRESIDENT.

Eligibility? Same as for President.

Term of office? Four years.

How elected? By the Presidential Electors, or by the United States Senate should the electors fail to make a choice.

Does he rank next to the President in power and responsibility? He does not.

What is his only duty? To act as President of the Senate.

What power has he in the Senate? As he is not a member of that body he can only discuss questions considered in committee of the whole, and has no vote except in case of a tie.

CIVIL GOVERNMENT.

Who was the first Vice-President? John Adams.

How many Vice-Presidents were re-elected? Four.

Name them. John Adams, George Clinton, Daniel D. Tompkins and John C. Calhoun.

How many have been elected President? Three; John Adams, Thomas Jefferson and Martin VanBuren.

How many have succeeded to the Presidency? Four; Tyler, Filmore, Johnson and Arthur. Which one was elected by the Senate? R. M. Johnson, of Kentucky, in 1837.

Previous to 1886 in case of death, removal, resignation or inability of both President and Vice-President, who succeeded to the Presidency? First, the president *pro tempore* of the Senate; next, the Speaker of the House of Representatives.

What bill was passed in 1886? The "Presidential Succession Bill."

What does it provide? That the members of the Cabinet shall succeed to the Presidency after the Vice-President.

Name the order of succession? Secretary of State, Treasury, War, Attorney General, Post Master General, Secretary of the Navy, Secretary of the Interior.

Salary of Vice-President? $8,000 per annum.

CHAPTER XII.

PRESIDENTIAL ELECTIONS.

How often do we elect a President? Once in four years.

What years are election years? All those exactly divisible by four.

When is the presidential election held? On the first Tuesday after the first Monday in November, next preceding the expiration of a presidential term.

Do the people vote directly for President and Vice-President? They do not.

For whom do they vote? For electors who vote for and elect President and Vice-President.

How are electors nominated? Each political party nominates its own electors.

How are they elected? By the people by a plurality vote.

Should there be more than one set of electors, which set would be elected? The set receiving the highest number of votes.

Do these electors consider that they are instructed for whom to vote? They do.

Have they ever dared to violate these instructions? They have not.

Under the Constitution would they have a right to vote for any other than the proposed candidates for President and Vice-President? They would.

To what does the number of electors correspond? To the number of members in both branches of Congress.

How many electors in the Electoral College of the United States? 401.

What part is necessary to a choice? A majority.

How many electors or electoral votes has Kentucky? Thirteen.

Why? Because she has eleven Congressmen and two United States Senators.

When were the first electors elected? In January, 1789.

When are they elected now? On the first Tuesday after the first Monday in November next preceding the expiration of a presidential term.

When was this time for holding presidential elections fixed by Congress? In 1845.

When and where do the electors of the several States meet and cast their votes for President and Vice-President? Formerly on the first Wednesday in December following their election at their respective State capitols, or such other places as might be designated by their State Legislatures, but now they meet on the second Monday in January.

When they have met how do they proceed? They cast separate votes by ballot for President and Vice-President, one of which shall not be from the same State as themselves, and make out three lists of the same, which are signed, sealed and certified to.

What do they do with these lists? They send one by mail to the President of the United States Senate, and one is sent to him by a special messenger, and the third is placed in the hands of the judge of the Federal Court of the district in which they meet.

When are these votes counted? On the second Wednesday in February following.

How? By the President of the Senate in the presence of both Houses of Congress.

In case no candidate has received a majority of the electoral votes what is done? The House of Representatives proceeds to elect a President from among the three having the highest number of votes.

How often has this been done? Three times; first, in the choice of Jefferson in 1801; next, in the choice of John Quincy Adams in 1825, and R. B. Hayes in 1877.

Should the House fail to make a choice by the 4th of March, who would become President? The Vice-President recently chosen either by the electors or by the Senate.

In the election of Vice-President by the Senate, who are voted for? The two candidates having the highest number of electoral votes.

In such elections how many shall constitute a quorum? Two-thirds of the whole number of Senators.

How many necessary to a choice? A majority of all the Senators.

Is the election of a President by the electoral vote an equitable one? It is not.

Why? Because the voice of the majority of the citizens is often suppressed and the minority rule the majority.

Give an instance? In 1860 Mr. Lincoln received a majority of fifty-seven electoral votes over all his competitors, while they received a popular majority over him of more than 900,000; also Hayes was chosen President while Tilden, his opponent, received a popular majority of 251,000; also in the recent election Harrison received a large majority of the electoral vote, while Cleveland received a popular majority of more than 100,000.

What is the cause of this inequality and injustice? It is owing to the superior relative power in the electoral college of the smaller States over the larger ones.

Illustrate. Delaware is entitled to one elector for her one Representative, and by virtue of her two Senators she is entitled to two more, thus, by her Senatorial equality, increasing her electoral power 200 per cent. New York is entitled to thirty-four electors for her thirty-four Representatives, and to only two more for her Senators, thus increasing her electoral power less than *six* per cent.

How may this injustice be removed? By so amending the Constitution as to elect a President by the popular vote.

CHAPTER XIII.

INAUGURATION, APPOINTMENTS, ETC.

When is the President inaugurated? On the 4th of March next following his election, provided the same does not fall on Sunday.

What Presidents have been inaugurated on Monday, the 5th of March? Jefferson in 1801, Jackson in 1829, Buchanan in 1857, and Cleveland in 1885.

How often does this occur? Once every twenty-eight years, or every seventh term.

What do you mean by inauguration? Taking the oath of office.

Who administers it? The Chief Justice.

What is said of this oath? It is very short and impressive.

What is he sworn to do? To preserve, protect and defend the Constitution of the United States to the best of his ability.

What is said of the appointing power of the President? It is very great and would be appalling were it not for the fact that the Senate has to approve and confirm said appointments.

How many appointments are made by the President direct? Probably 10,000.

How many are made indirectly, through the heads of departments? Probably 75,000.

Name some of the principal appointments made by the President. The Cabinet, or heads of departments, Justices of the Supreme Court and foreign ministers.

When are these appointments acted upon by the Senate? As soon as they are made, if it is in session; if not, said appointees, serve until it meets again, when they are either confirmed or rejected.

Of what does the President's Cabinet consist? The heads of departments, who are his counselors and advisers.

Would it be possible for the President to execute the laws and carry the government into successful operation without his Cabinet? It would not.

Can the President overrule or disregard the advice of his Cabinet? He can.

How many members in the Cabinet? Eight, viz., six Secretaries at the head of their respective departments of State, Treasury, War, Navy, Interior and Agriculture, the Post Master General and Attorney General.

Under Washington's administration, how many departments were there? Five, viz., State, Treasury, War, Post Office and Attorney General.

How many Cabinet officers were there? Three, viz., Secretary of State, Treasury and War.

When was the department of the Navy added? In 1798, and the Secretary became the fourth Cabinet officer.

When did the Post Master General become a Cabinet officer? In 1829, making the fifth.

When was the Attorney General made a Cabinet officer and the number raised to six? In 1841.

When was the Department of the Interior created and its chief given the seventh seat? In 1849.

When was the Department of Agriculture created? In 1862.

When was its Secretary made a Cabinet officer? In 1889.

When the departments are sub-divided what are these sub-divisions called? Bureaus; as the Bureau of Education, Bureau of Indian affairs, Pension Bureau, &c., &c.

CHAPTER XIV.

DEPARTMENT OF STATE.

Who is first in rank and importance of the Cabinet officers? The Secretary of State.

Who is Secretary of State at this time (1889)? Jas. G. Blaine.

How are the duties and business of Secretary of State divided? Into domestic and foreign affairs.

What is his first great duty under domestic affairs?

To keep and affix the Great Seal to all commissions signed by the President.

What besides the Great Seal is he required to keep in his office? The original copies of all acts, resolutions and orders of Congress.

What further is he required to do with these acts, etc.? To deliver a printed copy of them to each Senator and Representative, and to the Governor of each State.

What is the object of this? That each officer may know what changes have been made in the laws.

What is the duty of the Secretary of State respecting amendments to the Constitution? To publish and officially proclaim them.

What respecting treaties? He shall also publish and proclaim them.

What is his duty at the close of each session of Congress? He must cause to be published eleven thousand copies of all the laws, etc., of Congress.

What must he do with them? Distribute them.

To whom are they distributed? To the President, Vice-President, ex-Presidents, Senators and Representatives, heads of the departments, foreign ministers, to the judges, clerks and marshals of the United States Courts, etc.

What is done with the remainder? They are distributed among the States and Territories according to the number of their Representatives in Congress.

Enumerate some of his duties under foreign affairs?

He has charge of the diplomatic corps, carries on the correspondence with our foreign ministers and transacts the business with the ministers from foreign countries to the United States.

By whose advice is this correspondence carried on? The President's.

Who receives diplomats and foreign ministers to the United States? The President or Secretary of State.

What is a diplomat? A foreign minister.

What is a foreign minister? An agent sent by one government to transact business with another.

What are ministers sometimes called? Ambassadors.

CHAPTER XV.

FOREIGN MINISTERS.

How many classes of foreign ministers have we? Six.

Name them. Three classes of Envoys Extraordinary and Ministers Plenipotentiary, and one class each of Ministers Resident, Charge'd Affairs and Consuls General.

What determines the rank of a minister? The power with which he is clothed, the importance of the nation to which he is sent, and the salary he receives.

What do you mean by plenary? Full.

What do you mean by potens? Power.

What do you mean by plenipotentiary? Having full power.

To what countries are first class Envoys Extraordinary and Ministers Plenipotentiary sent? Great Britain, France, Germany and Russia.

What is their salary? $17,500 per annum.

Where are second class Ministers sent? To China,

Japan, Austro-Hungary, Italy, Brazil and Mexico.

What is their salary? $12,000.

Where are third-class sent? To Peru, Chili and the Central American States.

What is their salary? $10,000.

Where are fourth class or Ministers Resident sent? Argentine Republic, United States of Columbia, Spain, the Netherlands, &c.

What is their salary? $7,500.

Where are fifth class or Charge'd Affairs sent?

Switzerland, Norway and Sweden, Portugal &c.

What is their salary? $5,000.

Where are sixth class or Consuls General sent? They are sent to the principal cities of the world, viz., London, Paris, Vienna, St. Petersburg, Constantinople, &c.

What salary do they receive? From $6,000 down to $2,000 per annum.

What are their duties? To look after our commerce, vessels, seamen, property of deceased citizens of the United States, &c.

What are Secretaries of the Legation? Secretaries to the foreign ministers.

What power is sometimes conferred upon them? Power to act in the ministers' stead.

How are affairs of sudden and vital importance negotiated? By special ministers.

What are such commonly called? Commissioners.

How is the Secretary of State and the other Cabinet officers appointed? By the President by and with the advice and consent of the Senate.

CIVIL GOVERNMENT. 59

What salary do they receive ? $8,000 per annum.

CHAPTER XVI.

DEPARTMENT OF THE TREASURY.

What is the head of this department called? Secretary of the Treasury.

What are his duties and business? To oversee all the financial transactions of the Federal Government.

What of its rank and importance? By many it is considered higher than that of Secretary of State, and it requires the wisest, shrewdest and best men of the nation to fill it.

Upon what depends the success of every government, military movement, educational, commercial, industrial, or fraternal institution? A well managed and replete treasury.

Name some of the assistants of the Secretary of the Treasury. Two Assistant Secretaries, a Comptroller, several Auditors, a Comptroller of the Currency, a Treasurer, Register, Commissioner of Customs, Commissioner of Internal Revenue and several Bureaus, such as of Statistics, the Mint, Printing and Engraving, &c.

What of the Assistants and clerical force of this entire department? It is greater than any other department and costs the government annually about three million dollars to maintain it.

What is responsible for the hundreds of millions of bank notes used in the business of the country? The treasury of the United States.

What of our bank notes with such security as this? They are just as good as gold.

Who has oversight of the millions and millions of dollars paid into and out of our treasury? The Secretary of the Treasury.

About how much is paid into it annually? About four hundred millions.

Give the principal sources whence it comes? Tariff, Internal Revenue and sale of public lands.

How much is derived from the tariff? About two hundred and nineteen millions.

How much from Internal Revenue? About one hundred and twenty-four millions.

How much from sale of public lands? About eleven millions.

Where does the balance come from? Miscellaneous sources, such as sale of stamps, licenses, fines, forfeitures, &c.

How much is paid out of the treasury annually to carry on the *civil* government? Seventy-three millions.

How much for pensions? About a hundred millions.

How much for interest on public debt? About forty-five millions.

What was the public debt in 1789? Seventy-five millions.

When was it the smallest? In 1837 when it was only three hundred and thirty-seven thousand.

What was the financial condition of the country then? Times were hard and money was scarce.

When was the public debt the greatest? In 1866, when it was more than $2,773,000,000

What of the financial condition of the country then?

CIVIL GOVERNMENT. 61

Money was plentiful but its purchasing power was not very great.

What is the public debt at the present (1889)? Nearly $1,700,000,000.

How much to maintain the army? Thirty-nine millions.

The navy? Seventeen millions.

Indian affairs? Six millions.

CHAPTER XVII.

WAR DEPARTMENT.

Who is Commander in Chief of the army? The President.

Who ranks next to him in power and authority? The Secretary of War.

What is his rank in the Cabinet? It is the third in importance.

Over what has he control? The army and its affairs.

Name some of the officers of the bureaus of this department? Adjutant-General, Quartermaster-General, Paymaster-General, Chief of the Signal Service, &c.

How large a standing army has the United States at present? Twenty-six thousand.

How large is Russia's standing army? 975,000, or about thirty-six times as large as that of the United States.

What is the war footing of the United States? 3,165,000.

What do you mean by war footing? The number of men subject to military duty.

What can you say of this? It is larger than that of any other nation.

How many men were called into service by the Federal Government during the civil war? About three million.

How many did Kentucky furnish? Seventy-five thousand.

Where are most of the army officers educated and trained? In the Military Academy at West Point, N. Y.

Under what control is this? Control of Congress.

What is the object of the signal service? To make scientific observations and forecasts of the weather.

Why is this placed under the war department? Their widely scattered posts render it easy for them to manage.

The following is a part of the pay-roll and shows the rank and pay of the principal officers of the army:

OFFICER.	SALARY.
General	$13,500 per year.
Lieut. General	11,000 "
Major General	7,500 "
Brigadier General	5,500 "
Colonel	3,500 "
Lieut. Colonel	3,000 "
Major	2,500 "
Captain, mounted	2,000 "
Captain, not mounted	1,800 "
Regimental Adjutant	1,800 "
Regimental Quartermaster	1,800 "
First Lieutenant, mounted	1,600 "
" " not mounted	1,500 "
Second " mounted	1,500 "
" " not mounted	1,400 "
Chaplain	1,500 "

CHAPTER XVIII.

NAVY DEPARTMENT.

What is the Navy Department? The ship or war vessel department.

What is its chief officer called? Secretary of the Navy.

What does he have charge of? All the officers, men and war vessels pertaining to the navy of the United States.

How many vessels in our navy? About 140.

How many war vessels has Russia? 386.

How many vessels were added to our navy during the civil war? 400.

What was the highest number we had during that period? About 600.

How many men of all ranks in the United States navy? Eleven thousand.

How does the Secretary manage so many vessels and men and such a vast amount of property? Through the various bureaus.

Enumerate them? The Bureau of Yards and Docks, of Equipment and Recruiting, of Navigation, of Ordnance, of Medicine and Surgery, of Provisions and Clothing, of Steam Engineering, and of Construction and Repair.

Over what does the Bureau of Navigation have supervision? Over all that relates to the geography of the sea, the naval observatory, the nautical almanac and naval apprentices.

CIVIL GOVERNMENT.

Where are naval officers educated and trained? At the United States Naval Academy at Annapolis, Maryland.

The following is a partial list of the rank and pay of naval officers at sea:

OFFICERS.	SALARY.
Admiral	$13,000
Vice-Admiral	9,000
Rear-Admiral	6,000
Commodore	5,000
Captain	4,500
Commander	3,500

CHAPTER XIX.

INTERIOR DEPARTMENT.

When was this Department established? In 1849.

For what purpose? To relieve the other departments and further aid the President in the manipulation of the constantly increasing home affairs.

Into how many bureaus is this department divided? Six.

Name them. Patents, Public Lands, Indian Affairs, Pensions, the Census and Bureau of Education.

From what department was the Bureau of Patents transferred? From the Department of State.

The Bureau of Public Lands? From the Treasury Department.

The Bureau of Indian Affairs? From the War Department.

The Pension Bureau? From the War and Navy Departments.

The Census Bureau? From the Department of State.

Whom should you address to obtain a patent? The Commissioner of Patents, who will instruct you how to proceed.

Papers guaranteeing you a patent are called what? Letters Patent.

How are they signed? By the Secretary of the Interior and countersigned by the Commissioner of Patents and affixed with the seal of his office.

How would you obtain Public Lands? Apply to the Register of the Land Office in the district in which your claim is located and he will instruct you how to proceed.

What is the chief officer of the Bureau of Indian Affairs called? The Commissioner of Indian Affairs.

What is his business? He resides at Washington City and has oversight of the various superintendents, agents and sub-agents who reside near or among the Indians.

What is the duty of these agents and sub-agents? To receive and distribute the goods and money given by treaty to each tribe, and to oversee the schools and mechanical and industrial institutions established among the Indians.

Are Indians citizens and counted among our population? Except a few who are taxed they are not.

What is a pension? A provision made by the general government for the officers and privates of the army and navy disabled in the service of their country.

Who has charge of the Pension Bureau? The Commissioner of Pensions.

By whom is he appointed? By the President and the Senate.

What are his duties? To carry into effect the pension laws and to appoint pension agents in all the States and Territories.

What are the duties of these pension agents? To receive and distribute the money due pensioners, and to give information concerning pensions.

What is the chief of the Census Bureau called? The Superintendent of the Census.

What is the census? An enumeration or counting of the inhabitants of any country.

How often is our census taken? Once in every ten years.

What is the principal object in taking the census? To obtain the number of representatives each State is entitled to.

What besides the number of inhabitants is obtained by the census? The number of acres of land under cultivation, number of bushels of grain raised, number of horses, cattle, sheep, hogs, &c., number of manufacturing establishments and the amount of their productions, number of churches, schools, colleges &c., number of deaf, blind and insane persons, and a variety of other miscellaneous and valuable matter.

Who are designated by law as the persons to take the census? The United States Marshals.

Whom do the marshals appoint? A number of assistant marshals.

What is required of these assistant marshals? To

visit every house in their respective districts and obtain the number of persons and other statistical information.

How does he take down or register this information? On blanks.

Who prepares and prints these blanks and forwards them to the marshals? A board in the Interior Department appointed for that purpose.

Are these assistant marshals under oath? They are.

Are the citizens also sworn when they give in their lists? They are.

Should they fail to give a true list or refuse to answer the questions, what is the penalty? A fine of thirty dollars for each offense.

To whom do these assistants make their returns? The United States Marshals, who forward same to the superintendent, who formulates and publishes them.

What are the duties of the Commissioner of Education? To collect and publish information showing the condition and progress of schools in the States and Territories, and to publish any information that might promote the cause of education.

CHAPTER XX.

POST OFFICE DEPARTMENT.

What is the head of this department called? Post Master General.

What is his term of office and when does it begin? Four years, and begins one month after the inauguration of the President and continues one month after the expiration of a presidential term.

How many assistants has he? Three.

How designated? As first, second and third assistants.

What are the duties of the Post Master General? To maintain a general supervision over all the post office business of the United States.

What are the duties of the first assistant? He has charge of the Appointment Office and attends to all appointments and bonds given by post masters, agents and clerks, salaries and allowances where they are not provided for by law, free delivery in cities, blanks and reports, foreign postage, &c.

What are the duties of the Second Assistant? He has charge of the Contract Office, and attends to the letting of contracts and the transportation of mails, time schedules, mail equipments, maps and diagrams of mail routes, general distribution, &c.

What are the duties of the Third Assistant? He has charge of the Finance Office.

What two divisions in this office? Finance and Dead Letter.

Of what does the finance office have charge? The entire cash receipts, transfers and disbursements of the department, of postage stamps, stamped envelopes, newspaper wrappers and postal cards, registered letters and seals.

What are dead letters? Those not taken out of the office to which they were sent.

How long must a letter be advertised before it is sent to the dead letter office? Three weeks.

CIVIL GOVERNMENT.

What is done with letters at that office? They are opened and returned to the sender, if they contain his name and address.

If the rightful owner can not be discovered, how long are they held subject to his order? Four years.

What is done at the end of four years? Money or any articles of value they may contain is deposited in the treasury to the credit of the department.

By whom are the Post Master General and his assistants appointed? By the President and Senate.

Who are first, second and third class post masters? Those whose salary is a thousand dollars or more.

By whom are they appointed? The President.

Who are fourth and fifth class? Those whose salaries are less than a thousand dollars per year.

By whom are they appointed? By the Post Master General.

What is first class mail matter? All letters and all other written matter, sealed, nailed, sewed, tied or fastened so it can not be easily examined.

What is the rate of postage on first class matter? Two cents per ounce or fraction thereof.

What is second class mail matter? Only that usually sent by publishers of papers and news agents.

Rate of postage? One cent per pound.

What is third class mail matter? Printed matter in unsealed wrappers only.

What does this include? Books, circulars, chromos, engravings, handbills, lithographs, magazines, music, newspapers, pamphlets, photographs, proof sheets and manuscript accompanying the same, and in short any reproduction upon paper by any process except hand writing and the copying press.

Rate of postage on same? One cent for each two ounces or fraction thereof.

Limit of weight? Four pounds, except for a single book which may weigh more.

What is fourth class mail matter? All mailable matter not included in the three preceding classes, which is so prepared as to be easily withdrawn from the package and examined.

Rate of postage? One cent per ounce or fraction thereof.

Limit of weight? Four pounds.

What is the postage on letters to most foreign countries? Five cents on each letter.

What is the postage on newspapers? One cent for each two ounces.

Is the postage on mail matter going to Canada the same as in the United States? It is.

CHAPTER XXI.
ATTORNEY GENERAL.

What is the duty and business of the Attorney General? To give legal advice to the President when necessary, to institute suits for the United States and to defend suits against the same.

Who is the attorney of the Supreme Court? The Attorney General.

Of what officers has he charge? United States District Attorneys and Marshals.

CIVIL GOVERNMENT. 71

Name his principal assistants? Solicitor General, Assistant Attorney General, Assistant Attorney General at Court of Claims, Assistant Attorney General in the Interior Department, Assistant Attorney General in the Post Office Department.

What is this department called? The Department of Justice.

DEPARTMENT OF AGRICULTURE.

What is the head of this department called? Secretary of Agriculture.

When was he made a Cabinet officer? In 1889.

What is his business? To superintend the public and experimental grounds at Washington, to collect and distribute valuable seeds, to investigate contagious diseases of animals, to report the depredations of birds and noxious insects and to give such information as may be valuable to agriculturists and horticulturists.

PROMISCUOUS QUESTIONS.

What is the first day of our fiscal year? The first day of July.

What does fiscal mean? "Pertaining to the public treasury or revenue."

When are the fiscal reports of the departments made? June the 30th.

What of the President's pardoning power? He has power to grant reprieves and pardons for offenses against the United States, except in cases of impeachment.

What of his power in making treaties? He can make treaties by and with the advice and consent of the Senate, provided two-thirds of the Senators concur in the same.

What of his power to fill vacancies? He has power to fill vacancies during the recess of the Senate by granting commissions which shall expire at the end of their next session.

What is said about giving Congress information regarding legislation? He shall recommend such measures to their consideration as he shall deem necessary.

What of his power to convene and adjourn Congress? On extraordinary occasions he may convene both Houses or either of them; in case of disagreement between them with respect to time of adjournment, he may adjourn them to such time as he may see proper.

Has the President ever convened Congress in extra session? He has, more than once.

When? First in 1809, next in 1837 and again in 1861.

What are the last injunctions in the Constitution relative to the duties of the President? That he shall take care that the laws are faithfully executed, and shall commission all the officers of the United States.

CHAPTER XXII.

JUDICIAL DEPARTMENT.

What is the third branch of the government? The Judicial Department.

What is its sphere? To interpret the Constitution, to decide controversies, to try offenders and pronounce sentence upon them, to enforce rights, to keep the whole organism of the government in proper place and proportion.

What is this department sometimes called? A regulator of the governmental machinery, or the keystone of the government.

By the Constitution where is the judicial power of the United States vested? In the Supreme Court and such inferior courts as Congress may from time to time ordain and establish.

What is the highest tribunal in the United States? The Supreme Court.

By what is it ordained and established? By the CONSTITUTION.

By what is it organized? By Congress.

Name the inferior courts established and organized by Congress? United States Circuit Courts, District Courts, Court of Claims, Territorial Courts and the Courts of the District of Columbia.

The following diagram exhibits the various Federal or United States Courts together with their officers:

ONE SUPREME COURT.

1 Chief Justice $\left\{\begin{array}{l}\text{Clerks}\\\text{Marshal}\\\text{Repo't'r}\end{array}\right.$ $\left\{\begin{array}{l}\text{Attorney General.}\\ \\\text{Solictor General.}\end{array}\right.$
8 Associate Justices

NINE CIRCUIT COURTS.

8 Justices of Supreme Court $\left\{\begin{array}{l}\text{Clerks.}\\\text{District Marshals.}\\\text{District Attorneys.}\end{array}\right.$
9 Circuit Judges

FIFTY-SEVEN DISTRICT COURTS.

57 District Judges { Clerks, Marshals, Grand and Petit Juries } District Attorneys.

ONE COURT OF CLAIMS.

1 Chief Justice
4 Associate Justices } Clerks and Bailiff.

TERRITORIAL COURTS.

Judges { Marshals, Clerks } Attorneys.

COURTS OF THE DISTRICT OF COLUMBIA.

1 Chief Justice
4 Associate Justices } Marshal, Attorney, Clerk.

What are the officers of the United States Courts called? Judges, Attorneys, Marshals, Clerks, and in some cases a Reporter.

How are the judges of all these courts appointed? By the President and Senate.

Term of office? For life or during good behavior.

Why for life? To leave them free from dependence upon any other department and secure them against party influence.

How may their offices become vacant? By death, resignation or impeachment.

How are attorneys and marshals appointed? By the President and Senate.

Term of office? Four years.

What are the duties and business of the attorneys? They are the lawyers for the United States, and it is their business to prosecute all delinquents for crimes and offenses cognizable by the United States, and to represent the United States in all the civil actions occurring in their respective districts.

What are their duties respecting the Collectors of Customs and other revenue officers? They must defend them when suits are brought against them in their official capacity.

What must they report to the Solicitor of the Treasury? The number of suits determined and pending in their respective districts.

Their compensation? Their fees.

What are the duties of the Marshal? Similar to those of the sheriff of a county; he must serve all writs, orders, notices and processes given to him, make all arrests, attend the sittings in his district courts and keep order, pay off the jurors, &c.

What property is he custodian of? All vessels and goods seized by any revenue officer.

Is he under oath and bond? He is.

How is he assisted? By deputies chosen by himself.

What is his duty relative to the census? He appoints his assistants and distributes among them the blanks, and also receives them again and returns them to the Chief of the Census Bureau.

What is required of him on the first day of January and July each year? To make a return of all fees and emoluments of his office to the Secretary of the Interior.

Should they amount to more than $6,000 per year what must be done with the surplus? He must pay it into the United States Treasury.

By whom are the Clerks appointed? By the courts to which they belong.

Their duties? To keep a record of all orders and proceedings of the court and perform such other duties as shall devolve upon them.

Compensation? Their fees, except clerk of the Supreme Court, who gets $6,000 per year.

May the same clerk serve both the District and Circuit courts? He may.

CHAPTER XXIII.
THE SUPREME COURT.

Of what is the Supreme Court composed? Of one Chief Justice, eight Associate Justices, Attorney General, Solicitor General, Marshal, Clerk and Reporter.

Where and when does it meet? In Washington City, annually, on the first Monday in December.

How many judges constitute a quorum? Six.

What of the rank and precedence of the Associate Justices? They rank according to the date of their commissions, the earliest commission taking precedence of all the others.

What is the salary of the Chief Justice? $10,500, payable monthly out of the treasury.

Of the Associate Justices? $10,000, payable the same way.

Who are the Attorneys of the Supreme Court? The Attorney General and the Solicitor General.

Who is the Marshal? The Marshal of the District of Columbia.

How is the Reporter of the Supreme Court appointed? By the Court.

What are his duties? To note down and to have published the decisions and proceedings of the Court within eight months after the sitting of the Court.

His salary? $7,500.

Jurisdiction of Supreme Court? It has both original and appellate jurisdiction.

Over what cases has it original jurisdiction? Cases affecting foreign ministers and consuls and those in which a State shall be a party.

Over what cases has it appellate jurisdiction? Over such as have been appealed from the lower courts.

What do you mean by original jurisdiction? If a case can be instituted or brought in any court, that court is said to have original jurisdiction.

What do you mean by appellate jurisdiction? Jurisdiction over cases appealed from lower courts.

What is meant by exclusive jurisdiction? When a suit can be instituted only in a certain court.

UNITED STATES CIRCUIT COURTS.

What courts rank next in dignity, power and jurisdiction to the Supreme Court? The United States Circuit Courts.

Into how many Circuit Court districts are the United States divided? Nine.

Name the States composing the Sixth District? Tennessee, Kentucky, Ohio, Michigan.

Are these districts permanent? No, they are subject to change by Congress.

What is the design of these Circuit Courts? They are branches of the Supreme Court, and the object is to make them pervading and accessible to all the States.

When was the law creating circuit judges enacted? In 1869.

How many circuit judges are there? Nine; one for each Circuit Court district.

How does he hold his courts? Either alone or with the district judge as associate.

In case of his absence how may the court be held? By a district judge or by two district judges.

How often is a judge of the Supreme Court required to hold court in each circuit? At least once in two years.

Who may sit with him as associate? Either the circuit judge or the district judge.

What is the salary of a circuit judge? $6,000 per year.

What kinds of jurisdiction have the Circuit Courts? Original, appellate and concurrent.

What is meant by concurrent jurisdiction? Equal jurisdiction.

In what cases have they concurrent jurisdiction with the State Courts? In all cases where the matter in dispute exceeds the sum of $500 and the United States are plaintiffs, or where an alien is a party, or where the suit is between citizens of different States.

Over what matters have they exclusive jurisdiction?

Over all cases of crimes against the United States, except where the law especially confers the power on other courts.

Who acts as attorney for the circuit courts? The district attorney of the district in which the court is held.

Who is the Marshal? The United States Marshal of the district in which the court is held.

CHAPTER XXIV.
DISTRICT COURTS.

How do the District Courts rank? They are next in power and authority to the Circuit Courts.

Into how many United States Court districts are the United States divided? Fifty-seven.

What of the size of these districts? Every State constitutes at least one district; some are divided into two and some into three districts.

How many districts in Kentucky? Kentucky forms one district called "Kentucky district."

How many district judges? Fifty-seven; one to each district.

What are their salaries? From $3,500 to $5,000.

Who are the other officers? The District Attorney, the United States Marshal and Clerk.

Over what cases have the District Courts concurrent jurisdiction with the Circuit Courts? Over cases against consuls and vice-consuls where the amount does not exceed $100, and over all cases of crimes against the laws of the United States, not punishable by death.

Over what causes have they exclusive jurisdiction? Over all admiralty and maritime causes.

What is an admiral? The highest naval officer.

What are the laws respecting ships of war and warlike operations at Sea called? Laws of Admiralty.

What are the laws respecting vessels engaged in commercial affairs called? Maritime laws.

To what besides the operations at sea do these laws apply? The vessels on lakes and navigable rivers.

Then under what jurisdiction are all of our steamboats and steamboatmen? That of the United States District Court.

COURT OF CLAIMS.

Of what does the Court of Claims consist? Of one Chief Justice and four Associate Justices.

Their salaries? $4,500 per year.

When and where does this court hold its sessions? In Washington beginning on the first Monday in December each year and continues its sessions as long as business requires.

What is the mode of commencing proceedings before this court? By petition.

What is the object and business of this court? To save time of Congress and to adjust claims before they are presented to Congress; if this court allows a claim Congress will pass a bill for the benefit of the claimant.

TERRITORIAL COURTS.

Where are the Territorial Courts used? In the Territories for their government.

How divided? Into a Supreme Court and District Court.

What of the term of office of the judges of these courts? They are generally appointed for four years but may be removed sooner.

COURTS OF THE DISTRICT OF COLUMBIA.

Of what is the Supreme Court of this District composed? Of one Chief Justice and four Associate Justices.

When and where held? On the first Monday in December, in Washington City.

For what purpose? For the local government of the District of Columbia.

JURIES.

How many kinds of juries are there? Two; Grand Juries and Petit Juries.

In what kind of cases does the Grand Jury act? In criminal cases only.

In what kind does the Petit Jury act? In both criminal and civil cases.

The finding or conclusion of a Grand Jury is called what? A presentment or indictment.

What is the finding of a Petit Jury called? Its verdict.

Where does a Grand Jury sit? Alone, not in the presence of the court, and deliberates upon matters of a criminal character only.

What do you mean by the presentment or indictment of a Grand Jury? That they have found upon examination that a certain person has violated the law, and they present him to the court and call the attention of the officers to these violations, and recommend that judicial proceedings shall be instituted against him.

Does the Grand Jury ever try a case? It does not.

Where does a Petit Jury sit? With the court; hears the evidence, the pleading and arguing of the counsel and the instruction of the judge.

What do they then do? Retire to their room and deliberate alone.

After deliberation, if they agree, what do they do? If in a criminal case they bring in a verdict of "guilty or not guilty;" if in a civil case they say how much one party, if any, is indebted to the other.

Do these same questions relative to juries apply to the State courts? They do.

What provision respecting the retirement of Judges of the Federal Courts? They may retire after they are seventy years of age and still draw the same salary as at the time of their resignation.

POPULATION, &c., OF THE UNITED STATES, 1888.

STATES.	Estimated Population.	Popular Vote.	U. S. Senators.	Congressmen	Electoral Vote.
Alabama	1,500,000	174,100	2	8	10
Arkansas	1,140,000	155,968	2	5	7
California	1,350,000	251,339	2	6	8
Colorado	350,000	91,798	2	1	3
Connecticut	670,000	153,978	2	4	6
Delaware	150,000	29,787	2	1	3
Florida	450,000	66,641	2	2	4
Georgia	1,752,711	142,939	2	10	12
Illinois	3,750,000	747,686	2	20	22
Indiana	2,500,000	536,949	2	13	15
Iowa	1,800,000	404,140	2	11	13
Kansas	1,518,552	331,172	2	7	9
Kentucky	2,200,000	344,781	2	11	13
Louisiana	1,100,000	115,744	2	6	8
Maine	660,139	128,250	2	4	6
Maryland	1,100,000	210,921	2	6	8
Massachusetts	2,078,625	344,448	2	12	14
Michigan	2,195,692	475,313	2	11	13
Minnesota	1,250,000	263,306	2	5	7
Mississippi	1,300,000	115,807	2	7	9
Missouri	2,750,000	523,198	2	14	16
Nebraska	1,400,000	202,622	2	3	5
Nevada	61,000	12,632	2	1	3
New Hampshire	346,000	90,833	2	2	4
New Jersey	1,463,404	303,701	2	7	9
New York	6,500,000	1,320,109	2	34	36
North Carolina	1,650,000	285,473	2	9	11
Ohio	4,500,000	841,941	2	21	23
Oregon	250,000	61,911	2	1	3
Pennsylvania	5,400,000	997,568	2	28	30
Rhode Island	304,284	40,766	2	2	4
South Carolina	1,350,700	79,561	2	7	9
Tennessee	1,700,000	303,736	2	10	12
Texas	2,060,000	357,513	2	11	13
Vermont	333,000	63,440	2	2	4
Virginia	1,700,000	304,093	2	10	12
West Virginia	800,000	159,188	2	4	6
Wisconsin	1,700,000	354,614	2	9	11
Total	63,393,107	11,388,088	76	325	401

COMPARATIVE GOVERNMENTS

Country.	Kind of Government.	EXECUTIVE DEPARTMENT.		
		Executive	Term of Office	How Elected.
U. S. of America	Democratic Republic	President	4 years	By the People
Russia	Absolute Monarchy	Czar	For life	Hereditary
Great Britain	Limited Monarchy	King or Queen	For life	Hereditary
Germany	Limited Monarchy	Kaiser or Emperor	For life	Hereditary
France	Republic	President	7 years	By Senate and House of Deputies
Italy	Limited Monarchy	King or Queen	For life	Hereditary
Brazil	Limited Monarchy	Emperor	For life	Hereditary
Mexico	Republic	President	4 years	By electors
Canada	Appendage of Great Britain	Governor General	Indefinite	Appointed by the Crown
China	Absolute Mon.	Emperor	For life	Hereditary

CIVIL GOVERNMENT.
OF DIFFERENT COUNTRIES.

	LEGISLATIVE DEPARTMENT.						
Upper Branch	No. of Members.	Term of Office.	How Elected.	Lower Branch	No. of Members.	Term of Office.	How Elected.
Senate	76	6 yrs.	By the State Legislatures	House of Representatives	325	2 yrs	By the people
House of Lords	492	For life	Hereditary	House of Commons.	654	2 yrs	By the people
Bundesrath or Fed'l Council	59	1 yr.	By the States	Reichstag	397	3 yrs	By the people
Senate	225 and 75	9 yrs For life	By Dep'rt's and Colonies. By Nat'l Assembly	House of Deputies.	532	2 yrs	By the people
Senate		For life	Appointed by the King	Chamber of Deputies.	508	5 yrs	By the people
Senate		For life	By the popular vote	Congress		4 yrs	By the people
Senate		6 yrs.	By the State Legislatures	House of Deputies.		2 yrs	By the people
Senate	77	For life	By the Gov. General	House of Commons	206	2 yrs	By the people

86   CIVIL GOVERNMENT.

PRESIDENTIAL DIRECTORY.

Name.	Politics.	When elected.	Elect. vote received.	Total electoral vote.	Popular vote for.	Popular vote against.	Total popular vote.	Public Debt.
Geo. Washington	Federalist	1789	69	73				$ 75,463,476
Geo. Washington	Federalist	1792	132	135				77,217,924
Jno. Adams	Federalist	1796	71	138				83,702,172
Thos. Jefferson	Republican	1800	73	138				82,976,294
Thos. Jefferson	Republican	1804	162	176				86,427,120
James Madison	Republican	1808	122	176				65,196,317
James Madison	Republican	1812	128	218				45,209,737
James Monroe	Democratic Republican	1816	183	221				137,334,933
James Monroe	Republican	1820	231	235				91,015,566
Jno. Quincy Adams	Nat. Republican	1824	84	261				90,269,777
Andrew Jackson	Democrat	1828	178	261	647,231	509,097	1,156,328	67,475,043
Andrew Jackson	Democrat	1832	219	288	687,502	563,297	1,250,799	24,322,235
Martin Van Buren	Democrat	1836	170	294	761,549	730,676	1,492,205	336,957
Wm. H. Harrison	Whig	1840	234	294	1,275,017	1,135,761	2,410,778	5,250,875
Jas. K. Polk	Democrat	1844	170	275	1,337,243	1,361,268	2,698,611	23,401,652
Zachary Taylor	Whig	1848	163	290	1,360,101	1,511,807	2,871,908	47,044,862
Franklin Pierce	Democrat	1852	254	296	1,601,474	1,536,718	3,138,192	66,199,341
Jas. Buchanan	Democrat	1856	174	296	1,838,169	2,215,798	4,953,967	31,972,537
Abraham Lincoln	Modern Republican	1860	180	303	1,866,352	2,810,501	4,076,853	64,842,287
Abraham Lincoln	Republican	1864	212	314	2,216,067	1,808,725	4,024,792	1,815,784,370
U. S. Grant	Republican	1868	214	317	3,015,071	2,709,613	5,724,684	2,611,687,851
U. S. Grant	Republian	1872	286	366	3,597,071	2,869,090	6,466,161	2,253,251,328
R. B. Hayes	Republican	1876	185	369	4,033,295	4,375,527	8,408,822	2,180,395,067
Jas. A. Garfield	Republican	1880	214	369	4,450,921	4,765,933	9,216,854	2,128,791,054
Grover Cleveland	Democrat	1884	219	401	4,911,017	5,133,968	10,044,985	1,838,904,607
Benj. Harrison	Republican	1888	233	401	5,439,853	5,941,179	11,381,032	1,680,917,706

COMMITTEES OF THE SENATE.

STANDING COMMITTEES.

Committee on Agriculture and Forestry, on Appropriations, to Audit and Control the Contingent Expenses of the Senate, on Civil Service and Retrenchment, on Claims, on Commerce, on the District of Columbia, on Education and Labor, on Engrossed Bills, on Enrolled Bills, on Epidemic Diseases, to Examine the Several Branches of the Civil Service, on Expenditures of Public Money, on Finance, on Fisheries, on Foreign Relations, on the Improvement of the Mississippi River and its Tributaries, on Indian Affairs, on the Judiciary, on the Library,* on Manufactures, on Military Affairs, on Mines and Mining, on Naval Affairs, on Patents, on Pensions, on Post Offices and Post Roads, on Printing,* on Private Land Claims, on Privileges and Elections, on Public Buildings and Grounds,* on Public Lands, on Railroads, on the Revision of the Laws of the United States, on Revolutionary Claims, on Rules, on Territories, on Transportation Routes to the Seaboard.

*These committees have power to act concurrently with the same committees of the House of Representatives.

NOTE.—Questions unusual, or of special importance are generally considered by special or select committees appointed incidentally for the purpose.

CIVIL GOVERNMENT.

COMMITTEES OF THE HOUSE.

STANDING COMMITTEES.

Committees on Elections, on Ways and Means, on Appropriations, on the Judiciary, on Banking and Currency, on Coinage, on Weights and Measures, on Commerce, on Rivers and Harbors, on Agriculture, on Foreign Affairs, on Military Affairs, on Naval Affairs, on Post Offices and Post Roads, on the Public Lands, on Indian Affairs, on the Territories, on Railways and Canals, on Manufactures, on Mines and Mining, on Public Buildings and Grounds, on Pacific Railroads on, Levees and Improvements of the Mississippi River, on Education, on Labor, on the Militia, on Patents, on Invalid Pensions, on Pensions, on Claims, on War Claims, on Private Land Claims, for the District of Columbia, on the Revision of the Laws, on Expenditures in the Department of State, on Expenditures in the Treasury Department, on Expenditures in the War Department, on Expenditures in the Navy Department, on Expenditures in the Post Office Department, on Expenditures in the Interior Department, on Expenditures in the Department of Justice, on Expenditures on Public Buildings, on the Rules, on Accounts, on Mileage, Joint Committee on the Library, Joint Committee on Printing, on Enrolled Bills.

THE
Declaration of Independence.

DECLARED JULY 4, 1776.

WHEN, in the course of human events, it becomes necessary for one people to dissolve the political bands which have connected them with another, and to assume among the Powers of the earth, the separate and equal station to which the Laws of Nature and of Nature's God entitle them, a decent respect to the opinions of mankind requires that they should declare the causes which impel them to the separation.

We hold these truths to be self-evident: that all men are created equal; that they are endowed by their Creator with certain unalienable Rights; that among these are Life, Liberty and the pursuit of Happiness. That to secure these rights Governments are instituted among Men, deriving their just powers from the consent of the governed. That whenever any Form of Government becomes destructive of these ends, it is the Right of the People to alter or to abolish it, and to institute a new Government, laying its foundation on such principles and organizing its powers in such form, as to them shall seem most likely to effect their Safety and Happiness. Prudence, indeed, will dictate that Governments long established should not be changed for light and transient causes; and accordingly all experience hath shown that mankind are more disposed to suffer, while evils are sufferable, than to right themselves by abolishing the forms to which they are accustomed. But when a long train of abuses and usurpations, pursuing invariably the same Object, evinces a Design to reduce them under absolute Despotism, it is their right, it is their duty, to throw off such Government, and to provide new Guards for their future security. Such has been the patient sufferance of these Colonies; and such is now the necessity which constrains them to alter their former Systems of Government. The history of the present King of Great Britain is a history of repeated injuries and usurpations, all having in direct object the establishment of an absolute Tyranny over these States. To prove this, let Facts be submitted to a candid world.

He has refused his Assent to Laws the most wholesome and necessary for the public good.

He has forbidden his Governors to pass Laws of immediate and pressing importance, unless suspended in their operation till his Assent should be obtained; and when so suspended, he has utterly neglected to attend to them.

He has refused to pass other Laws for the accommodation of large districts of people, unless those people would relinquish the right of Representation in the Legislature, a right inestimable to them and formidable to tyrants only.

He has called together legislative bodies at places unusual, uncomfortable, and distant from the repository of their Public Records, for the sole purpose of fatiguing them into compliance with his measures.

He has dissolved Representative Houses repeatedly, for opposing with manly firmness his invasions upon the rights of the people.

He has refused for a long time, after such dissolutions to cause others to be elected, whereby the Legislative Powers, incapable of Annihilation, have returned to the people at large for their exercise; the State remaining in the meantime exposed to all the dangers of invasion from without, and convulsions within.

He has endeavored to prevent the population of these States; for that purpose obstructing the Laws for the Naturalization of Foreigners; refusing to pass others to encourage their migration hither, and raising the conditions of new Appropriations of Lands.

He has obstructed the Administration of Justice, by refusing his Assent to Laws for establishing Judiciary Powers.

He has made Judges dependent upon his Will alone, for the tenure of their offices, and the amount and payment of their salaries.

He has erected a multitude of New Offices, and sent hither swarms of Officers to harass our People and eat out their substance.

He has kept among us, in times of peace, Standing Armies without the Consent of our legislatures.

He has affected to render the Military independent of and superior to the Civil Power.

He has combined with others to subject us to a jurisdiction foreign to our constitution, and unacknowledged by our Laws; giving his Assent to their Acts of pretended Legislation :

For quartering large bodies of armed troops among us ;

For protecting them, by a mock Trial, from Punishment for any Murders which they should commit on the Inhabitants of these States ;

For cutting off our Trade with all parts of the world;

For imposing taxes upon us without our consent ;

For depriving us in many cases, of the benefits of Trial by Jury ;

For transporting us beyond Seas to be tried for pretended offenses ;

For abolishing the free System of English Laws in a neighboring Province, establishing therein an Arbitrary government, and enlarging its Boundaries so as to render it at once an example and fit instrument for introducing the same absolute rule into these Colonies;

For taking away our Charters, abolishing our most valuable Laws, and altering fundamentally the Forms of our Government;

For suspending our own Legislatures, and declaring themselves invested with Power to legislate for us in all cases whatsoever;

He has abdicated Government here by declaring us out of his Protection and waging war against us:

He has plundered our seas, ravaged our Coasts, burnt our towns, and destroyed the lives of our people.

He is at this time transporting large armies of foreign mercenaries to complete the works of death, desolation and tyranny, already begun with circumstances of Cruelty, and perfidy scarcely paralleled in the most barbarous ages, and totally unworthy the Head of a civilized nation.

He has constrained our fellow Citizens taken captive on the high Seas to bear arms against their Country, to become the executioners of their friends and Brethren, or to fall themselves by their Hands.

He has excited domestic insurrections amongst us, and has endeavored to bring on the inhabitants of our frontiers, the merciless Indian Savages, whose known rule of warfare is an undistinguished destruction of all ages, sexes and conditions.

In every stage of these Oppressions We have Petitioned for Redress in the most humble terms. Our repeated Petitions have been answered only by repeated injury. A Prince whose character is thus marked by every act which may define a Tyrant, is unfit to be the ruler of a free People.

Nor have we been wanting in attention to our British brethren. We have warned them from time to time of attempts by their legislature to extend an unwarrantable jurisdiction over us. We have reminded them of the circumstances of our emigration and settlement here. We have appealed to their native justice and magnanimity, and we have conjured them by the ties of common kindred to disavow these usurpations, which would inevitably interrupt our connections and correspondence. They too have been deaf to the voice of justice and of consanguinity. We must, therefore, acquiesce in the necessity which denounces our Separation, and hold them, as we hold the rest of mankind, Enemies in War, in Peace Friends.

We, therefore, the Representatives of the United States of America, in General Gongress Assembled, appealing to the Supreme Judge of the world for the rectitude of our intentions, do, in the Name, and by the Authority of the good people of these Colonies, solemnly publish and declare, That these United Colonies are, and of Right ought to be Free, and independent States; that they are Absolved from all Allegiance to the British Crown, and that all political connection between them and the State of Great Britain, is and ought to be totally dissolved; and that as free and Independent States, they have full Power to levy war, conclude Peace, contract Alliances, establish Commerce, and to do all other Acts and Things which Independent States may of right do. And for the support of this Declaration, with a firm reliance on the Protection of Divine Providence, we mutually pledge to each-other our Lives our Fortunes and our sacred Honor.

JOHN HANCOCK.

NEW HAMPSHIRE.—Josiah Bartlett, William Whipple, Matthew Thornton.

MASSACHUSETTS BAY,—Samuel Adams, John Adams, Robert Treat Paine, Elbridge Gerry.

RHODE ISLAND, ETC.—Stephen Hopkins, William Ellery.

CONNECTICUT.—Roger Sherman, Samuel Huntington, William Williams, Oliver Wolcott.

NEW YORK.—William Floyd, Phillip Livingston, Francis Lewis, Lewis Morris.

NEW JERSEY.—Richard Stockton, John Witherspoon, Francis Hopkinson, John Hart, Abraham Clark.

PENNSYLVANIA.—Robert Morris, Benjamin Rush, Benjamin Franklin, John Morton, George Clymer, James Smith, George Taylor, James Wilson, George Ross.

DELAWARE.—Cæsar Rodney, George Read, Thomas M'Kean.

MARYLAND.—Samuel Chase, William Paca, Thomas Stone, Charles Carroll, of Carrollton.

VIRGINIA.—George Wythe, Richard Henry Lee, Thomas Jefferson, Benjamin Harrison, Thomas Nelson, Jr., Francis Lightfoot Lee, Carter Braxton.

NORTH CAROLINA.—William Hooper, Joseph Hewes, John Penn.

SOUTH CAROLINA.—Edward Rutledge, Thomas Heyward, Jr., Thomas Lynch, Jr., Arthur Middleton.

GEORGIA.—Button Gwinnett, Lyman Hall, George Walton.

Articles of Confederation.

Articles of Confederation and Perpetual Union between the States of New Hampshire, Massachusetts Bay, Rhode Island and Providence Plantations, Connecticut, New York, New Jersey, Pennsylvania, Delaware, Maryland, Virginia, North Carolina, South Carolina and Georgia.

ARTICLE I. The style of this confederacy shall be, "The United States of America."

ART. II. Each State retains its sovereignty, freedom and independence, and every power, jurisdiction, and right which is not by this confederation expressly delegated to the United States in Congress assembled.

ART. III. The said States hereby severally enter into a firm league of friendship with each other, for their common defense, the security of their liberties, and their mutual and general welfare, binding themselves to assist each other against all force offered to, or attacks made upon them, or any of them, on account of religion, sovereignty, trade, or any other pretense whatever.

ART. IV. The better to secure and perpetuate mutual friendship and intercourse among the people of the different States in this Union, the free inhabitants of each of these States, paupers, vagabonds, and fugitves from Justice excepted, shall be entitled to all privileges and immunities of free citizens in the several States; and the people of each State shall have free ingress and regress to and from any other State, and shall enjoy therein all the privileges of trade and commerce, subject to the same duties, impositions and restrictions, as the inhabitants thereof respectively; provided that such restrictions shall not extend so far as to prevent the removal of any property imported into any State to any other State of which the owner is an inhabitant; provided, also, that no imposition, duties or restrictions, shall be laid on the property of the United States or either of them.

If any person guilty of, or charged with treason, felony, or other high misdemeanor in any State, shall flee from justice, and be found in any of the United States, he shall, upon demand of the governor or executive power of the State from which he fled, be delivered up and removed to the State having jurisdiction of his offense.

Full faith and credit shall be given in each of these States to the records, acts and judicial proceedings of the courts and magistrates of every other State.

ART. V. For the more convenient management of the general interest of the United States, delegates shall be annually appointed in such manner as the legislature of each State shall direct, to meet in Congress on the first Monday in November, in every year, with a power reserved to each State to recall its delegates, or any of them, within the year and send others in their stead for the remainder of the year.

No State shall be represented in Congress by less than two nor by more than seven members; and no person shall be capable of being a delegate for more than three years, in any term of six years; nor shall any person, being a delegate, be capable of holding any office under the United States for which he, or another for his benefit, receives any salary, fees, or emolument of any kind.

Each State shall maintain its own delegates in any meeting

of the States and while they act as members of the committee of the States.

In determining questions in the United States in Congress assembled, each State shall have but one vote.

Freedom of speech and debate in Congress shall not be impeached or questioned in any court or place out of Congress; and the members of Congress shall be protected in their persons from arrest and imprisonment during the time of their going to and from, and attendance on Congress, except for treason, felony or breach of the peace.

ART. VI. No State, without the consent of the United States, in Congress assembled, shall send any embassy to, or receive any embassy from, or enter into any conference, agreement, alliance, or treaty, with any king, prince or state; nor shall any person holding any office of profit or trust under the United States, or any of them, accept of any present, emolument, office or title of any kind whatever, from any king, prince, or foreign state; nor shall the United States, in Congress assembled, or any of them, grant any title of nobility.

No two or more States shall enter into any treaty, or confederation, or alliance whatever between them, without the consent of the United States, in Congress assembled, specifying accurately the purpose for which the same is to be entered into, and how long it shall continue.

No State shall lay any imposts or duties which may interfere with any stipulations in treaties entered into by the United States, in Congress assembled, with any king, prince, or state, in pursuance with any treaties already proposed by Congress to the courts of France or Spain.

No vessels of war shall be kept up in times of peace, by any State except such number only as shall be deemed necessary, by the United States, in Congress assembled, for the defense of such State or its trade; nor shall any body of forces be kept up, by any State, in time of peace, except such number only as, in the judgment of the United States, in Congress assembled, shall be deemed requisit to garrison the forts necessary for the defense of such State; but every State shall always keep up a well regulated and diciplined militia, sufficiently armed and accoutered, and shall provide and constantly have ready for use, in public stores, a due number of fieldpieces and tents, and a proper quantity of arms, ammunition, and camp equipage.

No State shall engage in any war without the consent of the United States, in Congress assembled, unless such State be actually invaded by enemies, or shall have received certain advice of a resolution being formed by some nation of Indians to invade such State, and the danger is so iminent as not to admit of a delay till the United States, in Congress assembled, can be consulted; nor shall any State grant commissions to any ship or vessel of war, nor letters of marque or reprisal, except it be after a declaration of war by the United States, in Congress assembled, and then only against the kingdom or state, and the subjects thereof against which war has been declared, and under such regulations as shall be established by the United States, in Congress assembled, unless such state be infested by pirates, in which case vessels of war may be fitted out for that occasion, and kept so long as the danger shall continue, or until the United States, in Congress assembled, shall determine otherwise.

ART. VII. When land forces are raised by any State for the common defense, all officers of or under the rank of colonel, shall be appointed by the legislature of each State respectively, by whom such forces shall be raised, or in such manner as such State shall direct, and all vacancies shall be filled up by the State which first made the appointment.

ART. VIII. All charges of war, and all other expenses that shall be incurred for the common defense or general welfare, and allowed by the United States, in Congress assembled, shall be defrayed out of a common treasury, which shall be supplied by the several States, in proportion to the value of all land within each State, granted to, or surveyed for, any person, as such land and the buildings and improvements thereon shall be estimated according to such mode as the United States, in Congress assembled, shall from time to time direct and appoint. The taxes for paying that proportion shall be laid and levied by the authority and direction of the legislatures of the several States, within the time agreed upon by the United States in Congress, assembled.

ART. IX. The United States, in Congress assembled shall have the sole and exclusive right and power of determining on peace and war, except in the cases mentioned in the Sixth Article; of sending and receiving ambassadors; entering into treaties and alliances, provided that no treaty of commerce shall be made whereby the legislative power of their respective States shall be restrained from imposing such imposts and duties on foreigners as their own people are subjected to, or from prohibiting the exportation or importation of any species of goods or commodities whatsoever; of establishing rules for deciding, in all cases, what captures on land or water shall be legal, and in what manner prizes taken by land or naval forces in the service of the United States, shall be divided or appropriated; of granting letters of marque and reprisal in time of peace; appointing courts for the trial of piracies and felonies committed on the high seas; and establishing courts for receiving and determining finaly appeals in all cases of captures; provided that no member of Congress shall be appointed a judge of any of the said courts.

The United States, in Congress assembled, shall also be the last resort on appeal, in all disputes and differences now subsisting, or that may hereafter arise between two or more States, concerning boundary, jurisdiction, or any other cause whatever; which authority shall always be exercised in the manner following: Whenever the legislative or executive authority, or lawful agent of any State in controversy with another, shall present a petition to Congress, stating the matter in question, and praying for a hearing, notice thereof shall be given by order of Congress, to the legislative authority of the other State in controversy, and a day assigned for the appearance of the other parties by their lawful agents, who shall then be directed to appoint, by joint consent, commissioners or judges to constitute a court for hearing and determining the the matter in question; but if they can not agree, Congress shall name three persons out of each of the United States, and from the list of such persons each party shall alternately strike out one, the petitioners beginning, until the number shall be reduced to thirteen; and from that number not less than seven nor more than nine names, as Congress shall direct, shall, in the presence of Congress be drawn, out by lot; and the persons whose names shall be drawn, or any five of them, shall be commissioners or judges, to hear and finally determine the controversy, so always as a major part of the judges, who shall hear the cause, shall agree in the determination; and if either party shall neglect to attend at the day appointed, without showing reasons which Congress shall judge sufficient, or being present, shall refuse to strike, then Congress shall proceed to nominate three persons out of each State, and the secretary of Congress shall strike in behalf of such party absent or refusing; and the judgment and sentence of the court, to be appointed in the manner before prescribed, shall be final and conclusive; and if any of the parties shall refuse to submit to the authority of such court, or to appear or defend their claim or cause, the court shall nevertheless proceed to pronounce sentence or judgment, which shall in like manner be final and decisive; the judgment or sentence and other proceedings being in either case transmitted to Congress, and lodged among the acts of Congress for the security of the parties concerned; provided, that every commissioner, before he sits in judgment, shall take an oath, to be administered by one of the judges of the supreme or superior court of the State where the cause shall be tried, "well and truly to hear and determine the matter in question, according to the best of his judgment, without favor, affection, or hope of reward." Provided, also, that no State shall be deprived of territory for the benefit of the United States.

All controversies concerning the private right of soil claimed under different grants of two or more States, whose jurisdictions, as they may respect such lands, and the States which passed such grants are adjusted, the said grants or either of them being at the same time claimed to have originated antecedent to such settlement of jurisdiction, shall, on the petition of either party to the Congress of the United States, be finally determined, as near as may be, in the same manner as is before prescribed for deciding disputes respecting territorial jurisdiction between different States.

The United States, in Congress assembled, shall also have the sole and exclusive right and power of regulating the alloy and value of coin struck by their own authority, or by that of the respective States; fixing the standard of weights and measures throughout the United States; regulating the trade and managing all affairs with the Indians not members of any of the States; provided that the legislative right of any State, within its own limits, be not infringed or violated; establishing and regulating post-offices from one State to another throughout all the United States, and exacting such postage on the papers passing through the same, as may be requisite to defray the expenses of the said office; appointing all officers of the land forces in the service of the United States, excepting regimental officers; appointing all the officers of the naval force, and commissioning all officers whatever in the service of the United States; making rules for the government and regulation of the said land and naval forces, and directing their operations.

The United States, in Congress assembled, shall have authority to appoint a committee, to sit in the recess of Congress, to be denominated "A Committee of the States," and to consist of one delegate from each State; and to appoint such other committees and civil officers as may be necessary for managing the general affairs of the United States under their direction; to appoint one of their number to preside provided that no person be allowed to serve in the office of president more than one year in any term of three years; to ascertain the necessary sums of money to be raised for the service of the United States, and to appropriate and apply the same for defraying the public expenses; to borrow money or emit bills on the credit of the United States, transmitting every half year to the respective States an account of the sums of money so borrowed or emitted; to build and equip a navy; to agree upon the number of land forces, and to make requisitions from each State for its quota, in proportion to the number of white inhabitants in such State, which requisition shall be binding; and thereupon the Legislature of each State shall appoint the regimental officers, raise the men, and clothe, arm, and equip them in a soldier-like manner at the expense of the United States; and the officers and men so clothed, armed and equipped shall march to the place appointed, and within the time agreed on by the United States, in Congress assembled; but if the United States, in Congress assembled, shall, on consideration of circumstances, judge proper that any State should not raise men, or should raise a smaller number than its quota, and that any other State should raise a greater number of men than the quota thereof, such extra number shall be raised, officered, clothed, armed, and equipped in the same manner as the quota of such State, unless the Legislature of such State shall judge that such extra number can not be safely spared out of the same, in which case they shall raise, officer, clothe, arm, and equip as many of such extra number as they judge can be safely spared, and the officers and men so clothed, armed, and equipped shall march to the place appointed, and within the time agreed on by the United States, in Congress assembled.

The United States, in Congress assembled, shall not engage in a war, nor grant letters of marque and reprisal in time of peace, nor enter into any treaties or alliances, nor coin money, nor regulate the value thereof, nor ascertain the sums and expenses necessary for the defense and welfare of the United States, or any of them, nor emit bills, nor borrow money on the credit of the United States, nor appropriate money, nor agree upon the number of vessels of war to be built or purchased, or the number of land or sea forces to be raised, nor appoint a commander-in-chief of the army or navy, unless nine States assent to the same, nor shall a question on any other point, except for adjourning from day to day, be determined, unless by the votes of a majority of the United States in Congress assembled.

The Congress of the United States shall have power to adjourn to any time within the year, and to any place within the United States, so that no period of adjournment be for a longer duration than the space of six months, and shall publish the journal of their proceedings monthly, except such parts thereof relating to treaties, alliances, or military operations as in their judgment require secrecy; and the yeas and nays of the delegates of each State, on any question, shall be entered on the journal, when it is desired by any delegate; and the delegates of a State or any of them, at his or their request, shall be furnished with a transcript of the said journal, except such parts as are above excepted, to lay before the legislatures of the several States.

ART. X. The committees of the States, or any nine of them, shall be authorized to execute, in the recess of Congress, such of the powers of Congress as the United States, in Congress assembled, by the consent of nine States, shall, from time to time, think expedient to vest them with; provided that no power be delegated to the said committees, for the exercise of which, by the articles of confederation, the voice of nine

States in the Congress of the United States assembled is requisite.

ART. XI. Canada acceding to this confederation, and joining in the measures of the United States, shall be admitted into, and entitled to all the advantages of this Union; but no other colony shall be admitted into the same unless such admission be agreed to by nine States.

ART. XII. All bills of credit emitted, moneys borrowed, and debts contracted by and under the authority of Congress, before the assembling of the United States, in pursuance of the present confederation, shall be deemed and considered as a charge against the United States, for payment and satisfaction whereof the said United States and the public faith are hereby solemnly pledged.

ART. XIII. Every State shall abide by the determinations of the United States, in Congress assembled, on all questions which by this Confederation are submitted to them. And the Articles of this Confederation shall be inviolably observed by every State, and the Union shall be perpetual; nor shall any alteration at any time hereafter be myde in any of them unless such alteration be agreed to in a Congress of the United States, and be afterwards confirmed by the legislatures of every State.

And whereas it hath pleased the great Governor of the world to incline the hearts of the legislatures we respectively represent in Congress, to approve of, and to authorize us to ratify the said Articles of Confederation and perpetual Union, Know ye, that we, the undersigned delegates, by virtue of the power and authority to us given for that purpose, do, by these presents, in the name and in behalf of our respective constituents, fully and entirely ratify each and every one of the said Articles of Confederation and perpetual Union, and all and singular the matters and things therein contained. And we do further solemnly plight and engage the faith of our respective constituents, that they shall abide by the determinations of the United States, in Congress assembled, on all questions which by the said Confederation are submitted to them; and that the Articles thereof shall be inviolably observed by the States we respectively represent, and that the Union shall be perpetual. In witness whereof, we have hereunto set our hands in Congress. Done at Philadelphia, in the State of Pennsylvania, the ninth day of July, in the year of our Lord 1778, and in the third year of the Independence of America.

The Constitution of the United States of America.

THE PREAMBLE.

"WE, the People of the United States, in order to form a more perfect union, establish justice, insure domestic tranquillity, provide for the common defense, promote the general welfare, and secure the blessings of liberty to ourselves and our posterity, do ordain and establish this Constitution for the United States of America."

ARTICLE I.

THE LEGISLATIVE DEPARTMENT.

Section I.—The Congress in General.

"All legislative power herein granted, shall be vested in a Congress of the United States, which shall consist of a Senate and House of Representatives."

Section II.—House of Representatives.

1. "The House of Representatives shall be composed of members chosen every second year by the people of the several States, and the electors in each State shall have the qualifications requisite for electors of the most numerous branch of the State legislature."

2. "No person shall be a Representative, who shall not

have attained the age of twenty-five years, and been seven years a citizen of the United States, and who shall not, when elected, be an inhabitant of that State in which he shall be chosen."

3. "Representatives and direct taxes shall be apportioned among the several States which may be included within this Union, according to their respective numbers, which shall be determined by adding to the whole number of free persons, including those bound to service for a term of years, and excluding Indians not taxed, three-fifths of all other persons. The actual enumeration shall be made within three years after the first meeting of the Congress of the United States, and within every subsequent term of ten years, in such manner as they shall by law direct. The number of Representatives shall not exceed one for every thirty thousand, but each State shall have at least one Representative; and until such enumeration shall be made, the State of New Hampshire shall be entitled to choose three, Massachusetts eight, Rhode Island and Providence Plantations one, Connecticut five, New York six, New Jersey four, Pennsylvania eight, Delaware one, Maryland six, Virginia ten, North Carolina five, South Carolina five and Georgia three."

4. "When vacancies happen in the representation from any State, the executive authority thereof shall issue writs of election to fill such vacancies."

5. "The House of Representatives shall choose their Speaker and other officers; and shall have the sole power of impeachment."

Section III.—The Senate.

1. "The Senate of the United States shall be composed of two Senators from each State, chosen by the Legislature thereof, for six years; and each Senator shall have one vote."

2. "Immediately after they shall be assembled, in consequence of the first election, they shall be divided as equally

as may be, into three classes. The seats of the Senators of the first class shall be vacated at the expiration of the second year; of the second class, at the expiration of the fourth year; and of the third class, at the expiration of the sixth year; so that one-third may be chosen every second year; and if vacancies happen by resignation, or otherwise, during the recess of the legislature of any State, the executive thereof may make temporary appointments until the next meeting of the legislature, which shall then fill such vacancies."

3. "No person shall be a Senator who shall not have attained the age of thirty years, and been nine years a citizen of the United States, and who shall not, when elected, be an inhabitant of that State for which he shall be chosen."

4. "The Vice-President of the United States shall be President of the Senate, but shall have no vote, unless they be equally divided."

5. "The Senate shall choose their other officers, and also a President *pro tempore*, in the absence of the Vice-President, or when he shall exercise the office of President of the United States."

6. "The Senate shall have the sole power to try all impeachments. When sitting for that purpose, they shall be on oath or affirmation. When the President of the United States is tried, the Chief-Justice shall preside; and no person shall be convicted without the concurrence of two-thirds of the members present."

7. "Judgment in cases of impeachment shall not extend further than to removal from office, and disqualification to hold and enjoy any office of honor, trust, or profit, under the United States; but the party convicted shall, nevertheless, be liable and subject to indictment, trial, judgment, and punishment, according to law."

Section IV.—*Both Houses.*

1. "The times, places, and manner of holding elections for

Senators and Representatives, shall be prescribed in each State by the Legislature thereof; but the Congress may at any time, by law, make or alter such regulations, except as to the places of choosing Senators."

2. "The Congress shall assemble at least once in every year, and such meeting shall be on the first Monday in December, unless they shall by law appoint a different day."

Section V.—*The Houses Separately.*

1. "Each House shall be the judge of the election, returns, and qualifications of its own members, and a majority of each shall constitute a quorum to do business ; but a smaller number may adjourn from day to day, and may be authorized to compel the attendance of absent members, in such manner, and under such penalties, as each House may provide."

2. "Each House may determine the rules of its proceedings, punish its members for disorderly behavior, and, with the concurrence of two-thirds, expel a member."

3. "Each House shall keep a journal of its proceedings, and, from time to time, publish the same, excepting such parts as may, in their judgment, require secrecy: and the yeas and nays of the members of either House, on any question, shall, at the desire of one-fifth of those present, be entered on the journal."

4. "Neither House, during the session of Congress, shall, without the consent of the other, adjourn for more than three days, nor to any other place than that in which the two Houses may be sitting."

Section VI.—*Privileges and Disabilities of Members.*

1. "The Senators and Representatives shall receive a compensation for their services, to be ascertained by law, and paid out of the Treasury of the United States. They shall, in all cases, except treason, felony, and breach of the peace, be privileged from arrest during their attendance at the session

of their respective Houses, and in going to, and returning from, the same; and for any speech or debate in either House, they shall not be questioned in any other place."

2. "No Senator or Representative shall, during the time for which he was elected, be appointed to any civil office under the authority of the United States, which shall have been created, or the emoluments whereof shall have been increased during such time; and no person, holding any office under the United States, shall be a member of either House during his continuance in office."

Section VII.—*Mode of Passing Laws.*

1. "All bills for raising revenue shall originate in the House of Representatives; but the Senate may propose or concur with amendments, as on other bills."

2. "Every bill which shall have passed the House of Representatives and the Senate, shall, before it becomes a law, be presented to the President of the United States; if he approve, he shall sign it, but if not, he shall return it, with his objections, to that House in which it shall have originated, who shall enter the objections at large on their journal, and proceed to reconsider it. If, after such reconsideration, two-thirds of that House shall agree to pass the bill, it shall be sent, together with the objections, to the other House, by which it shall likewise be reconsidered, and, if approved by two-thirds of that House, it shall become a law. But in all such cases the votes of both Houses shall be determined by yeas and nays, and the names of the persons voting for and against the bill shall be entered on the journal of each House, respectively. If any bill shall not be returned by the President within ten days (Sundays excepted) after it shall have been presented to him, the same shall be a law, in like manner as if he had signed it, unless the Congress, by their adjournment, prevent its return, in which case it shall not be a law."

3. "Every order, resolution, or vote, to which the concurrence of the Senate and House of Representatives may be necessary (except on a case of adjournment), shall be presented to the President of the United States; and before the same shall take effect, shall be approved by him, or, being disapproved by him, shall be repassed by two-thirds of the Senate and House of Representatives, according to the rules and limitations prescribed in the case of a bill."

Section VIII.—*Powers Granted to Congress.*

1. "The Congress shall have power to lay and collect taxes, duties, imposts,, and excises, to pay the debts and provide for the common defense and general welfare of the United States; but all duties, imposts, and excises shall be uniform throughout the United States."

2. "To borrow money on the credit of the United States."

3. "To regulate commerce with foreign nations, and among the several States, and with the Indian tribes."

4. "To establish a uniform rule of naturalization, and uniform laws on the subject of bankruptcies, throughout the United States."

5. "To coin money, regulate the value thereof, and of foreign coin, and fix the standard of weights and measures."

6. "To provide for the punishment of counterfeiting the securities and current coin of the United States."

7. "To establish post-offices and post-roads."

8. "To promote the progress of science and useful arts, by securing, for limited times, to authors and inventors, the exclusive right to their respective writings and discoveries."

9. "To constitute tribunals inferior to the Supreme Court."

10. "To define and punish piracies and felonies committed on the high seas, and offenses against the law of nations."

11. "To declare war, grant letters of marque and reprisal, and make rules concerning captures on land and water."

12. "To raise and support armies; but no appropriation

of money to that use shall be for a longer term than two years."

13. "To provide and maintain a navy."

14. "To make rules for the government and regulation of the land and naval forces."

15. "To provide for calling forth the militia to execute the laws of the Union, suppress insurrections, and repel invasions."

16. "To provide for organizing, arming, and disciplining the militia, and for governing such part of them as may be employed in the service of the United States; reserving to the States respectively, the appointment of the officers, and the authority of training the militia, according to the discipline prescribed by Congress."

17. "To exercise exclusive legislation in all cases whatsoever, over such district (not exceeding ten miles square), as may, by cession of particular States, and the acceptance of Congress, become the seat of the Government of the United States, and to exercise like authority over all places purchased by the consent of the legislature of the State in which the same shall be, for the erection of forts, magazines, arsenals, dockyards, and other needful buildings."

18. "To make all laws which shall be necessary and proper for carrying into execution the foregoing powers, and all other powers vested by this Constitution in the Government of the United States, or in any department or officer thereof."

Section IX.—*Powers denied to the United States.*

1. "The migration or importation of such persons as any of the States, now existing, shall think proper to admit, shall not be prohibited by the Congress, prior to the year one thousand eight hundred and eight; but a tax or duty may be imposed on such importation, not exceeding ten dollars for each person."

2. "The privilege of the writ of *habeas corpus* shall not be

suspended unless when, in cases of rebellion or invasion, the public safety may require it."

3. "No bill of attainder, or *ex post facto* law, shall be passed."

4. "No capitation or other direct tax shall be laid, unless in proportion to the *census* or enumeration, herein before directed to be taken."

5. "No tax or duty shall be laid on articles exported from any State."

6 "No preference shall be given by any regulation of commerce or revenue, to the ports of one State over those of another; nor shall vessels bound to, or from, one State, be obliged to enter, clear, or pay duties, in another."

7. "No money shall be drawn from the treasury, but in consequence of appropriations made by law; and a regular statement and account of the receipts and expenditures of all public money shall be published, from time to time."

8. "No title of nobility shall be granted by the United States; and no person, holding any office of profit or trust under them, shall, without the consent of the Congress, accept of any present, emolument, office, or title, of any kind whatever, from any king, prince, or foreign state."

Section X.—*Powers Denied to the Congress.*

1. "No State shall enter into any treaty, alliance, or confederation; grant letters of marque and reprisal; coin money; emit bills of credit; make anything but gold and silver coin a tender in payment of debts, pass any bill of attainder, *ex post facto* law, or law impairing the obligation of contracts, or grant any title of nobility."

2. "No State shall, without the consent of the Congress, lay any imposts or duties on imports or exports, except what may be absolutely necessary for executing its inspection laws; and the net produce of all duties and imposts, laid by any State on imports or exports, shall be for the use of the treas-

ury of the United States; and all such laws shall be subject to the revision and control of the Congress."

3. "No State shall, without the consent of Congress, lay any duty of tonnage, keep troops, or ships of war, in time of peace, enter into any agreement or compact with another State, or with a foreign power, or engage in war, unless actually invaded, or in such imminent danger as will not admit of delay."

ARTICLE II

THE EXECUTIVE DEPARTMENT.

Section I.—President and Vice-President.

1. "The Executive power shall be vested in a President of the United States of America. He shall hold his office during the term of four years, and together with the Vice-President, chosen for the same term, be elected as follows:"

2. "Each State shall appoint, in such a manner as the Legislature thereof may direct, a number of Electors, equal to the whole number of Senators and Representatives to which the State may be entitled in the Congress; but no Senator or Representative, or person holding an office of trust or profit under the United States, shall be appointed an Elector."

3. "The Electors shall meet in their respective States and vote by ballot for two persons, of whom one, at least, shall not be an inhabitant of the same State with themselves. And they shall make a list of all the persons voted for, and of the number of votes for each; which list they shall sign and certify, and transmit, sealed to the seat of the Government of the United States, directed to the President of the Senate. The President of the Senate shall, in the presence of the Senate and House of Representatives, open all the certificates, and the votes therein shall then be counted. The person having the greatest number of votes shall be President, if such number be a majority of the whole number of Electors appointed; and if there be more than one who have such a majority, and have

an equal number of votes, then the House of Representatives shall immediately choose, by ballot, one of them for President; and if no person have a majority, then, from the five highest on the list, the said House shall, in like manner, choose the President. But in choosing the President, the votes shall be taken by States, the representation from each State having one vote; a quorum for this purpose shall consist of a member or members from two-thirds of the States, and a majority of all the States shall be necessary to a choice. In every case, after the choice of the President, the person having the greatest number of votes of the Electors shall be Vice-President. But if there should remain two or more who have equal votes, the Senate shall choose from them, by ballot, the Vice-President."

4. "The Congress may determine the time of choosing the Electors, and the day on which they shall give their votes; which day shall be the same throughout the United States."

5. "No person, except a natural-born citizen, or a citizen of the United States at the time of the adoption of this Constitution, shall be eligible to the office of President; neither shall any person be eligible to that office who shall not have attained to the age of thirty-five years, and been fourteen years a resident within the United States."

6. "In case of the removal of the President from office, or of his death, resignation, or inability to discharge the powers and duties of the said office, the same shall devolve on the Vice-President, and the Congress may by law provide for the case of removal, death, resignation, or inability both of the President and Vice-President, declaring what officer shall then act as President, and such officer shall act accordingly, until the disability be removed, or a President shall be elected."

7. The President shall, at stated times, receive for his services, a compensation which shall neither be increased nor diminished during that period for which he shall have been

elected, and he shall not receive within that period any other emolument from the United States, or any of them."

8. "Before he enter on the execution of his office, he shall take the following oath or affirmation: 'I do solemnly swear (or affirm), that I will faithfully execute the office of President of the United States, and will, to the best of my ability, preserve, protect, and defend the Constitution of the United States.'"

Section II.—*Powers of the President.*

1. "The President shall be commander-in-chief of the army and navy of the United States, and of the militia of the several States, when called into active service of the United States; he may require the opinion, in writing, of the principal officer in each of the executive departments, upon any subject relating to the duties of their respective offices, and he shall have power to grant reprieves and pardons for offenses against the United States, except in cases of impeachment."

2. "He shall have power, by and with the advice and consent of the Senate, to make treaties, provided two-thirds of the Senators present concur; and he shall nominate, and by and with the advice and consent of the Senate, shall appoint ambassadors, other public ministers, and consuls, judges of the Supreme Court, and all other officers of the United States, whose appointments are not herein otherwise provided for, and which shall be established by law: but the Congress may by law vest the appointment of inferior officers, as they think proper, in the President alone, in the courts of law, or in the heads of Departments."

3. "The President shall have power to fill up all vacancies that may happen during the recess of the Senate, by granting commissions, which shall expire at the end of their next session."

Section III.—*Duties of the President.*

"He shall, from time to time, give to the Congress information of the State of the Union, and recommend to their consideration such measures as he shall judge necessary and expedient; he may, on extraordinary occasions, convene both Houses, or either of them, and in case of disagreement between them, with respect to the time of adjournment, he may adjourn them to such time as he shall think proper; he shall receive ambassadors and other public ministers; he shall take care that the laws be faithfully executed, and shall commission all the officers of the United States."

ARTICLE III.
JUDICIAL DEPARTMENT.

Section I.—United States Court.

"The judicial power of the United States shall be vested in one Supreme Court, and in such inferior courts as the Congress may, from time to time, ordain and establish. The judges, both of the Supreme and inferior courts, shall hold their offices during good behavior, and shall, at stated times, receive for their services a compensation, which shall not be diminished during their continuance in office."

Section II.—Jurisdiction of the United States Courts.

1. "The judicial power shall extend to all cases, in law and equity, arising under this Constitution, the laws of the United States, and treaties made, or which shall be made, under their authority; to all cases affecting ambassadors, other public ministers, and consuls; to all cases of admiralty and maritime jurisdiction; to controversies to which the United States shall be a party; to controversies between two or more States, between a State and citizens of another State, between citizens of different States, between citizens of the same State, claiming lands under grants of different States, and between a State or the citizens thereof, and foreign States, citizens, or subjects."

2. "In all cases affecting ambassadors, other public minis-

ters, and consuls, and those in which a State shall be a party, the Supreme Court shall have original jurisdiction. In all the other cases before mentioned, the Supreme Court shall have appellate jurisdiction, both as to law and fact, with such exceptions, and under such regulations, as the Congress shall make."

3. "The trial of all crimes, except in cases of impeachment, shall be by jury; and such trial shall be held in the State where the said crimes shall have been committed; but when not committed within any State, the trial shall be at such place, or places, as the Congress may by law have directed."

Section III.—Treason.

1. "Treason against the United States shall consist only in levying war against them, or adhering to their enemies, giving them aid and comfort. No person shall be convicted of treason, unless on the testimony of two witnesses to the same overt act, or on confession in open court."

2. "The Congress shall have power to declare the punishment of treason, but no attainder of treason shall work corruption of blood, or forfeiture, except during the life of the person attainted."

ARTICLE IV.

Section I.—State Records.

"Full faith and credit shall be given in each State to the public acts, records and judicial proceedings of every other State. And the Congress may, by general laws, prescribe the manner in which such acts, records, and proceedings shall be proved and the effect thereof.

Section II.—Privileges of the Citizens.

1. "The citizens of each State shall be entitled to all privileges and immunities of citizens in the several States."

2. "A person charged in any State with treason, felony, or other crime, who shall flee from justice, and be found in an-

other State, shall, on demand of the executive authority of the State from which he fled, be delivered up, to be removed to the State having jurisdiction of the crime."

3. "No person held to service or labor in one State, under the laws thereof, escaping into another, shall, in consequence of any law or regulation, be discharged from such service or labor, but shall be delivered up on claim of the party to whom such service or labor may be due."

Section III.—*New States and Territories.*

1. "New States may be admitted by the Congress into this Union; but no new State shall be formed, or erected, within the jurisdiction of any other State; nor any State be formed, by the junction of two or more States, or parts of States, without the consent of the legislatures of the States concerned, as well as of the Congress."

2. "The Congress shall have power to dispose of and make all needful rules and regulations respecting the territory or other property, belonging to the United States; and nothing in this Constitution shall be so construed as to prejudice any claims of the United States, or of any particular State."

Section IV.—*Guarantee to the States.*

"The United States shall guarantee to every State in this Union a republican form of government, and shall protect each of them against invasion; and on application of the legislature, or of the executive (when the legislature can not be convened), against domestic violence."

ARTICLE V.
Power of Amendment.

"The Congress, whenever two-thirds of both Houses shall deem it necessary, shall propose amendments to this Constitution, or, on the application of the legislatures of two-thirds of the several States, shall call a convention for proposing amendments, which, in either case, shall be valid to all intents and purposes, as part of this Constitution, when ratified by the legislatures of three-fourths of the several States, or by conventions in three-fourths thereof, as the one or the other mode of ratification may be proposed by the Congress; Provided, that no amendment, which may be made prior to the year one thousand eight hundred and eight, shall, in any manner, affect the first and fourth clauses in the ninth section of the first article; and that no State, without its consent, shall be deprived of its equal suffrage in the Senate."

ARTICLE VI.

Public Debt, Supremacy of the Constitution, Oath of Office, Religious Test.

1. "All debts contracted, and engagements entered into, before the adoption of this Constitution, shall be as valid against the United States, under this Constitution, as under the Confederation."

2. "This Constitution, and the laws of the United States which shall be made in pursuance thereof, and all treaties made, or which shall be made, under the authority of the United States, shall be the supreme law of the land; and the judges in every State shall be bound thereby, anything in the Constitution or laws of any State to the contrary notwithstanding."

3. "The Senators and Representatives before mentioned, and the members of the several State legislatures, and all executive and judicial officers, both of the United States, and of the several States, shall be bound by oath or affirmation, to support this Constitution, but no religious test shall ever be required as a qualification to any office or public trust under the United States."

ARTICLE VII.

Ratification of the Constitution.

"The ratifications of the Conventions of nine States shall

be sufficient for the establishment of this Constitution between the States so ratifying the same."

<small>Done in convention by the unanimous consent of the States present, the seventeenth day of September, in the year of our Lord, one thousand seven hundred and eighty-seven, and of the Independence of the United States of America the twelfth.</small>

AMENDMENTS TO THE CONSTITUTION.

Articles in Addition to, and Amendment of, the Constitution of the United States of America.

Proposed by Congress and ratified by the Legislatures of the several States, pursuant to the fifth article of the original Constitution.

Article I.—Freedom of Religion, etc.

"Congress shall make no law respecting an establishment of religion, or prohibiting the free exercise thereof, or abridging the freedom of speech, or of the press; or the right of the people peaceably to assemble, and to petition the Government for a redress of grievances."

Article II.—Right to Bear Arms.

"A well-regulated militia being necessary to the security of a free State, the right of the people to keep and bear arms shall not be infringed."

Article III.—Quartering Soldiers on Citizens.

"No soldier shall, in time of peace, be quartered in any house without the consent of the owner; nor, in time of war, but in a manner to be prescribed by law."

Article IV.—Search-Warrants.

"The right of the people to be secure in their persons, houses, papers, and effects, against unreasonable searches and seizures, shall not be violated; and no warrants shall issue, but upon probable cause, supported by oath or affirmation, and particularly describing the place to be searched, and the persons or things to be seized."

Article V.—Trial for Crime, etc.

"No person shall be held to answer for a capital or otherwise infamous crime, unless on a presentment or indictment of a grand jury, except in cases arising in the land or naval forces, or in the militia, when in actual service, in time of war, or public danger; nor shall any person be subject, for the same offense, to be twice put in jeopardy of life or limb; nor shall be compelled in any criminal case to be a witness against himself, nor be deprived of life, liberty, or property, without due process of law; nor shall private property be taken for public use, without just compensation."

Article VI.—Rights of Accused Persons.

"In all criminal prosecutions, the accused shall enjoy the right to a speedy and public trial, by an impartial jury of the State and district wherein the crime shall have been committed, which district shall have been previously ascertained by law, and to be informed of the nature and cause of the accusation; to be confronted with the witnesses against him; to have compulsory process for obtaining witnesses in his favor; and to have the assistance of counsel for his defense."

Article VII.—Suits at Common Law.

"In suits at common law, where the value in controversy shall exceed twenty dollars, the right of trial by jury shall be preserved; and no fact, tried by a jury, shall be otherwise reexamined in any court of the United States, than according to the rules of the common law."

Article VIII.—Excessive Bail.

"Excessive bail shall not be required, nor excessive fines imposed, nor cruel and unusual punishment inflicted."

Article IX.—Rights Retained by the People.

"The enumeration in the Constitution of certain rights shall not be construed to deny or disparage others retained by the people."

Article X.—Reserved Powers of the States.

"The powers not delegated to the United States by the Constitution, nor prohibited by it to the States, are reserved to the States respectively, or to the people."

Article XI.

"The judicial power of the United States shall not be construed to extend to any suit in law or equity, commenced or prosecuted against one of the United States by citizens of another State, or by citizens or subjects of any foreign State."

Article XII.—Mode of Choosing the President and Vice-President.

1 "The Electors shall meet in their respective States, and vote by ballot for President and Vice-President, one of whom, at least, shall not be an inhabitant of the same State with themselves; they shall name in their ballots the person voted for as President, and in distinct ballots the person voted for as Vice-President; and they shall make distinct lists of all persons voted for as President, and of all persons voted for as Vice-President, and of the number of votes for each, which lists they shall sign and certify, and transmit, sealed, to the seat of government of the United States, directed to the President of the Senate; the President of the Senate shall, in the presence of the Senate and House of Representatives, open

all the certificates, and the votes shall then be counted; the person having the greatest number of votes for President shall be the President, if such number be a majority of the whole number of Electors appointed; and if no person have such a majority, then from the persons having the highest number, not exceeding three, on the list of those voted for as President, the House of Representatives shall choose immediately, by ballot, the President. But in choosing the President, the votes shall be taken by States, the representation from each State having one vote; a quorum for this purpose shall consist of a member or members from two-thirds of the States, and a majority of all the States shall be necessary to a choice. And if the House of Representatives shall not choose a President, whenever the right to choose shall devolve upon them, before the fourth day of March next following, then the Vice-President shall act as President, as in case of the death, or other constitutional disability, of the President."

2. "The person having the greatest number of votes as Vice-President shall be the Vice-President, if such number be a majority of the whole number of Electors appointed; and if no person have a majority, then, from the two highest numbers on the list, the Senate shall choose the Vice-President; a quorum for the purpose shall consist of two-thirds of the whole number of Senators; a majority of the whole number shall be necessary to a choice."

3 "But no person constitutionally ineligible to the office of President, shall be eligible to that of Vice-President of the United States."

Article XIII.—*Abolition of Slavery.*

1. "Neither slavery or involuntary servitude, except as a punishment for crime, whereof the party shall have been duly convicted, shall exist within the United States or any place subject of their jurisdiction."

2. "Congress shall have power to enforce this article by appropriate legislation."

Article XIV.—*Right of Citizenship, etc.*

1. "All persons born or naturalized in the United States, and subject to the jurisdiction thereof, are citizens of the United States and of the State wherein they reside. No State shall make or enforce any law which shall abridge the privileges or immunities of citizens of the United States ; nor shall any State deprive any person of life, liberty, or property without due process of law, nor to deny to any person within its jurisdiction the equal protection of the laws.

2. "Representatives shall be apportioned among the several States according to their respective numbers, counting the whole number of persons in each State, excluding Indians not taxed. But when the right to vote at any election for the choice of Electors for President and Vice-President of the United States, Representatives in Congress, the executive and judicial officers of a State, or the members of the Legislature thereof, is denied to any of the male inhabitants of such State, being twenty-one years of age, and citizens of the United States, or in any way abridged, except for participation in rebellion or other crime, the basis of representation therein shall be reduced in the proportion which the number of such male citizens shall bear to the whole number of male citizens, twenty-one years of age, in such State.

3. "No person shall be a Senator or Representative in Congress, or Elector of President and Vice-President, or hold any office, civil or military, under the United States, or under any State, who, having previously taken an oath as a member of Congress, or as an officer of the United States, or as a member of any State Legislature, or as an executive or judicial officer of any State, to support the Constitution of the United States. shall have engaged in insurrection or rebellion against the same, or given aid or comfort to the enemies thereof. But

Congress may, by a vote of two-thirds of each House, remove such disability."

4. "The validity of the public debt of the United States, authorized by law, iucluding debts incurred for payment of pensions and bounties for services in suppressing insurrection or rebellion, shall not be questioned. But neither the United States nor any State shall assume or pay any debt or obligation in aid of insurrection or rebellion against the United States, or any claim for the loss or emancipation of any slave, but all such debts, obligations, and claims shall be held illegal and void."

5. "The Congress shall have power to enforce by appropriate legislation, the provisions of this article."

Article XV.—Right of Suffrage.

1. "The right of citizens of the United States to vote shall not be denied or abridged by the United States, or by any State, on account of race, color, or previous condition of servitude."

2. "The Congress shall have power to enforce this article by appropriate legislation."

Part Third.

CHAPTER I.

LOCAL GOVERNMENT.

Where is the Supreme power of the United States lodged? In the *general* government.

What is general government? A controlling power exercised over the whole people and pertaining to general interests.

What is local government? The government of a certain locality, pertaining to the interests or affairs of that locality only.

To what is the authority of the general government restricted? To the powers expressly conferred on it by the Constitution.

To what are all other powers reserved? To the States or to the people.

Are the States sovereign? They are in their own limits over all questions not expressly assigned to the general government.

In case of a conflict between a local and the general government which is the higher power? The general government.

Illustrate. The XIII, XIV and XV Amendments to the Constitution of the United States were in conflict with parts of some of the State Constitutions.

What was the effect? Those parts of the said State Constitutions became null and void.

What is the great aim and object of both kinds of government? The welfare of the people.

For what purpose do we elect Congressmen and United States Senators? To make laws for our general welfare, such as relate to national defense, national currency, post offices, transactions with foreign powers, &c.

For what purpose do we elect State Legislators? To make laws for our local or home affairs, such as relate to our public schools, charitable institutions, incorporation of our towns, development of our agricultural and mining interests, &c.

Is there not a great similarity between the general government and the State government? There is; the State governments are modeled after the United States government.

Point out the similarity in the divisions of the governments? The United States government is divided into Legislative, Executive and Judicial departments; so also are the State governments.

Show the similarity in the Executive departments? The United States has a President and Vice-President, while each State has a Governor and Lieutenant-Governor.

Show the similarity in the Legislative departments? The United States has a Congress divided into two branches, while the States have a Legislature divided into two branches.

Show the similarity of their Judicial departments? The United States has a Supreme Court, Circuit Court, District Court, &c., while each State has a Supreme Court, or Court of Appeals, Circuit Courts, County Courts, &c.

Are all the State governments similar? They are very much alike, and a knowledge of the government of one will suffice for the general principle of all.

CHAPTER II.

KENTUCKY.

What is the motto of Kentucky? "United we stand, divided we fall."

What is the sobriquet? "The dark and bloody ground."

What is it often called? The "Blue-grass State."

GEOGRAPHY.

What is the latitude of the southern boundary? 36° 30'.

What is the latitude of the northern boundary? 39° 06'.

Eastern limit of longitude? 5° W. from Washington.

Western limit of longitude? 12° 38' W. from Washington.

Give the boundary of the State of Kentucky? Beginning in the southeast corner at seven pines and two black oaks on the top of Cumberland mountains on the Tennessee line, where it crosses said mountains one mile and a half and twelve poles southwardly of Cumberland Gap, thence with Walker's old marked line S., 86° W. to Tennessee river, thence up and with the Tennessee river to Alexander and Munsell's line, thence with said line to the Mississippi river below New Madrid, thence up the channel of the Mississippi river to a point on the north bank of the Ohio river at its mouth, thence with the north bank of the Ohio river at low water mark to a point opposite the mouth of the Big Sandy river, thence across the Ohio river and up the said Sandy to the mouth of the main western branch of Sandy river, thence up the northwesterly branch to the intersection of a line drawn south 45° W., thence with said line to the beginning.

What is the length of the Tennessee border? 300 miles.

The Mississippi border? Fifty miles.

The Ohio border? 642 miles.

The Big Sandy border? 120 miles.

The mountain line? 130 miles.

Total boundary? 1,242 miles.

What is the greatest length of the State from East to West? 411 miles.

What is its extreme breadth? 179 miles.

Its area? About 40,000 square miles, or about 25,000,000 acres.

What was the population in 1885? 1,648,690.

Present population? About 2,200,000.

What is the altitude of the Western point at New

Madrid? 300 feet above the level of the sea.

What is the average altitude of the Eastern part? 1,600 feet above the sea.

What is the fall or difference of altitude between the Eastern and Western parts? 1,300 feet.

What the total length of river border? 733 miles.

How many miles of river within the State limits? More than 4,000.

How far does Kentucky's jurisdiction extend? To low water mark on the north bank of the Ohio river, and to the middle of the Mississippi, Tennessee, and Big Sandy Rivers.

CHAPTER III.

ORIGIN OF KENTUCKY.

Of what State was Kentucky originally part? Of Virginia.

Of what county in Virginia was it a part? Augusta county.

When was Augusta county, Virginia, organized? In 1738.

When was Augusta county divided and Botetourt (Bot-e-turt) county formed of part of the same? In 1769.

When was Botetourt county divided and Fincastle formed of a part of it? In 1772.

In those days what was the custom in the division of a county? If they divided a county into two counties one of them retained the original name, but if into three they dropped the original name.

When was Fincastle county divided into the counties

of Washington, Montgomery, and Kentucky? In 1776.

What was the Eastern boundary of Kentucky county? Big Sandy river.

What of the Western boundary? It was unlimited; not well defined.

When was Kentucky county, Virginia, divided into Fayette, Jefferson, and Lincoln counties (now Kentucky)? In 1781.

For how long was the name Kentucky dropped? Two years.

When were these three counties organized into Kentucky district? In 1783.

What kind of a district was this? A judicial district.

Why was it established? That they might have a court nearer than old Virginia.

How far were they from the settlements in old Virginia? Nearly 500 miles.

What did the settlers of Kentucky district painfully realize? That they sadly needed a local government of their own.

SEPARATION.

When were the first steps taken to separate Kentucky district from Virginia and organize it into a State and ask admittance into the Union? In 1784.

What was the nature of this separation? It was peaceable.

What are the articles of agreement called? "The compact with Virginia."

When was this compact made? December 18, 1789.

When did Congress pass an act to admit Kentucky into the Union? February 4, 1791.

How many conventions up to this time (1791) had the people held relative to their separation from Virginia and their admission into the Union? Nine.

How much time had elapsed? Seven years.

What was the cause of all this delay? Indian wars, the unsettled condition of affairs, and the impending change in the general government.

When were delegates elected to the tenth convention? December, 1791.

What convention was this? The one that ordained and established the first Constitution of Kentucky.

Who presided over this convention? Samuel McDowell, who had also presided over the other nine.

How many delegates in this convention? Forty-five.

How many counties in Kentucky at that time? Nine, and they sent five delegates each.

When and where did this convention meet? At Danville, April 3d, 1792.

When did they adopt and sign the first Constitution? April 19, 1792.

How many Constitutions has Kentucky had? Three.

When was Kentucky admitted into the Union? June 1st, 1792, at which time the government went into operation under the first Constitution.

CHAPTER IV.

FIRST CONSTITUTION.

When and where did the first Legislature of Kentucky convene? June the 4th, 1792, at Lexington.

Who had been chosen Governor by the College of Electors? Isaac Shelby.

What of Shelby? He and Garrard were the only men ever twice elected Governor of Kentucky.

Were his terms consecutive? They were not.

What was the first law made by the first legislature of Kentucky? "An Act establishing an Auditor's Office of Public Accounts."

When was it approved by the Governor and made a law? June 22, 1792. How long was the first session of the Legislature, and when did it adjourn? Twenty-five days, adjourned June 29, 1792.

Under the first Constitution how were the Governor and Senators chosen? By electors who were chosen by the people.

How was voting done? By ballot.

How many days did they hold elections? Three consecutive days.

Why? On account of the great distance the voters had to travel.

In what was the executive power vested? In a Governor only, as they had no Lieutenant-Governor.

In case of the death, resignation, or inability of the Governor, who took his place? The Speaker of the Senate.

How were the Representatives elected? By the people.

What two officers were also elected by the people? Sheriff and Coroner.

How were the Judges and Magistrates appointed? By the Governor.

For how long were the Judges appointed? For life, or during good behavior.

In case they were guilty of an offense, not justifying impeachment, how were they removed from office? On the address of two-thirds of each branch of the Legislature.

How was the Treasurer appointed? By joint ballot of both Houses of the Legislature.

What is the capitol of Kentucky? Frankfort.

When was it selected? In 1792.

How? The Legislature appointed twenty-one commissioners from various parts of the State, and the delegates from Mercer and Fayette counties were to strike out one name each alternately till the number was reduced to five, and these, or any three of them, were to name the place for seat of government.

When did Frankfort become the seat of government? In 1797.

How long did the government continue under this first Constitution? Eight years.

In what year were the people to have an opportunity to vote for a call of a convention to amend this Constitution? In 1797.

Was such a vote taken? It was.

What was the result? Five counties failed to report.

Was a vote taken the next year? There was.

What was the result? Ten counties failed to report.

What was then done? It was evident that the people were in favor of the calling of a convention, and the Legislature made the call by a two-thirds vote.

What followed? Delegates were elected by the people, who met at Frankfort and produced the second Constitution.

When was it signed? The 17th day of August, 1799.

When did it go into full force and effect? June 1st, 1800.

CHAPTER V.

SECOND CONSTITUTION.

What change of election days under this Constitution? A change from the first Tuesday in May to the first Monday in August.

What change of voting? From ballot to *viva voce*.

How often were Representatives elected? Annually.

How often were appointments made? Once in four years.

How were Senators elected? By the people.

Term of office? Four years.

Into how many classes were they divided? Four.

How were the Governor and Lieutenant-Governor elected? By the people.

Term of office? Four years.

Time of inauguration? Fourth Tuesday after the election.

Under this Constitution how long was the Governor ineligible? Seven years.

What of judges? They were still appointed, and held office the same as under the first Constitution.

What new courts were established? County Courts.

How were surveyors, coroners and justices of the

peace appointed? By the Governor, upon the recommendation of a majority of the magistrates.

How were clerks appointed? Each court appointed its own clerk, who held office for life or during good behavior.

How were sheriffs appointed? By the Governor, upon the recommendation of a majority of the magistrates; the sheriff was chosen from among the magistrates, and the one holding the oldest commission was made sheriff.

How were the Secretary of State and Attorney General appointed? By the Governor.

What was the stupendous feature of this Constitution? The appointive power of the Executive.

What change was made in the third Constitution? The appointive power was greatly diminished, and most all the offices were filled by elections by the people.

What was the oppressive feature of this Constitution? There was no limit to the power of the Legislature to borrow money on the credit of the State. The public debt at one time amounted to $4,500,000 nearly.

What restriction upon this in the present Constitution? The Legislature can not borrow more than $500,000 on the credit of the State.

How long was this Constitution in force and effect. Fifty years.

How was this Constitution to be amended, readopted or changed? By a convention called for that purpose.

Before such a convention could be called what was necessary to be done? To take the voice of the people on the subject for two consecutive years.

Who was ordered to take this vote? The sheriffs and other returning officers.

Under what authority was this done? That of the Legislature.

What time was prescribed by this Constitution for the Legislature to pass an act authorizing such a vote to be taken? Within twenty days after the Legislature convened.

By what vote? By a majority of each House.

In taking the vote who were counted in favor of calling a convention? Only those who voted affirmatively.

Who were counted against it? Not only those voting against it, but also those not voting at all.

What number was necessary to call the convention? A majority of all the citizens of the State entitled to vote for a Representative at each of the elections.

Should it appear that a majority of the voters were in favor of calling a convention, what must the Legislature at its next session do? Call a convention to consist of as many members as there were in the House of Representatives and no more.

How were these members or delegates chosen? In the same manner and proportion, and at the same time and places, as Representatives were.

When were said delegates required to meet? Within three months after their election, at the State Capitol.

When did the Legislature order an election for calling a convention to revise the second Constitution? In 1846.

When was the first election held? In 1847.

When the second? 1848.

What was the result of these two elections? The returns showed a majority in favor of calling a convention.

How many were in favor of it? About 102,000.

How many against it? About 40,000.

When did the Legislature pass the act calling the convention? June 13, 1849.

When did the convention assemble? October 1st, 1849.

What was the result of the deliberations of this convention? They ordained and established the present Constitution.

How long were they in session? About eight months.

When was it adopted? June 1st, 1850.

When did it go into force and effect? Immediately.

CHAPTER VI.

THIRD OR PRESENT CONSTITUTION.

Who ordained and established this Constitution? The people of the Commonwealth of Kentucky, through their delegates in convention assembled.

For what purpose? To secure to every citizen thereof the rights of "life, liberty, property, and the pursuit of happiness."

What sacred right is guaranteed to the people under this Constitution? The right to a voice in the selection of all public officers.

When was the first general election under this Constitution held? May the 12th, 1851.

What officers were for the first time in the history of Kentucky elected by the people? Appellate Judges, Clerk of the Court of Appeals, Circuit Judges, Commonwealth's Attorneys, and in each county a County Judge, County Attorney, County Clerk, Circuit Clerk, Sheriff, Jailer, Assessor, Surveyor, Justices of the Peace, and Constables.

How many branches of government are established by this Constitution? Three.

What are they? The Legislative, Executive and Judicial.

LEGISLATIVE DEPARTMENT.

In what is the legislative power vested? In the Legislature, or "General Assembly of Kentucky."

Of what is it composed? Of a Senate and House of Representatives.

What is its enacting clause? "Be it enacted by the General Assembly of the Commonwealth of Kentucky."

HOUSE OF REPRESENTATIVES.

How many members in the House of Representatives. One hundred.

Is this number subject to change or fixed? It is fixed by the Constitution.

How is representation apportioned? According to the number of qualified voters.

How often is an apportionment made? Once every eight years.

When was the second apportionment made? In 1857. The third? 1865.

The fourth? In 1873. The fifth? In 1881.

When will the sixth be made? In 1889.

How is representation equalized? The State is divided into ten districts, and the number of Representatives apportioned to each district according to the number of its voters.

In what district is this county? (See Article 2, Sec. 6 of Constitution).

Of how many counties is it composed? See same place.

How is the ratio or basis of representation ascertained? By dividing the whole number of voters in the State by 100, the whole number of Representatives.

How is the number of Representatives each district is entitled to, found? By dividing the whole number of qualified voters in the district by the ratio or basis of representation.

Should a county not have voters enough to entitle it to a Representative what is done? Two or more small counties are joined together.

When are Representatives elected? On the first Monday in August in the odd years.

How? By the qualified voters.

Who are the qualified voters, according to the Constitution? See Article 2 Sec. 8.

Eligibility of a Representative? He must be a voter and twenty-four years of age.

CHAPTER VII.
THE SENATE.

Of how many members is the Senate composed? Thirty-eight.

Does this number change, or is it permanent? It is fixed by the Constitution.

How are Senators apportioned? At each apportionment the State is divided into thirty-eight Senatorial Districts containing, as nearly as may be, an equal number of voters, provided a county shall not be divided and the counties composing each district shall be adjoining.

What Senatorial District is this? (See table of Senatorial Districts).

Of what counties is it composed? See same place.

Eligibility of a Senator? He must be a citizen of the United States, thirty years of age, a resident of the State six years next preceding his election, and the last year thereof of the district from which he is elected.

Term of office? Four years.

Into how many classes are they divided? Two.

When do the terms of one-half of them expire? Every two years.

What are those whose terms of office are unexpired called? Old, or held-over members.

How many are newly elected members each session? Nineteen (one-half).

What is the compensation of Senators and Representatives? They get the same amount, five dollars per day, $12\frac{1}{2}$ cents per mile mileage (each way), and twenty dollars for stationery.

How are vacancies filled? By special election.

Who are ineligible to membership in the General Assembly of Kentucky? See Article 2, Sections 26, 27, and 28.

CHAPTER VIII.

ORGANIZATION.

When does the General Assembly convene? On the first Monday in December in the odd years.

Is this date fixed? It is not, but may be changed by the Legislature as to time of the year.

How many members in each House constitute a quorum? A majority.

What may a smaller number do? Adjourn from day to day and compel the attendance of the other members.

What are the exclusive privileges of each house? To judge of its own election returns; to make its own standing rules; to punish its own members; to keep its own journal; to fix the time of its adjournment provided it does not exceed three days; to elect its own officers and to appoint its own committees.

Who organizes and presides over the Senate? The Lieutenant-Governor.

What is he called? Speaker of the Senate.

What are his privileges? When in committee of the whole, he may debate and vote on all subjects, and when the Senate is equally divided he may give the casting vote.

In case of death of the Lieutenant-Governor, or his removal or inability, or when he acts as Governor, what would the Senate do? Proceed to elect a Speaker *pro tempore* from among their number.

How are the committees appointed? By the Speaker, unless the Senate shall direct otherwise, in which case they are elected by a plurality vote.

How many standing committees has the Senate? Twenty-three.

What are the other officers of the Senate? Clerks, Sergeant-at-Arms and Doorkeeper.

Are they members? They are not.

Who appoints the pages, keeper of the cloak-room, janitor, and other attachees? The Sergeant-at-Arms.

HOUSE OF REPRESENTATIVES.

Who organizes the House of Representatives? The Clerk of the last House, who is furnished with a list of the members elect by the Secretary of State.

How does he proceed? Calls the House to order and has the oath of office administered to the members.

What is the next thing in order? The nomination and election of a Speaker.

What are his duties? To preside over the House and preserve order and decorum, to prove the journal and to appoint the standing and other committees.

How many standing committees has the House of Representatives? Twenty-nine.

What are the other officers of the House? Clerks, Sergeant-at-Arms and Doorkeeper.

How are they elected? They must be put in nomination and elected by a majority vote.

When the organization of both Houses is complete what do they do? Appoint a joint committee to notify the Governor that they are ready for business.

What does he do? Sends in his message.

What is done with this message? It is received, read,

and each item of business is referred to an appropriate standing committee.

What else is done with the message? It is printed, wrapped in stamped wrappers, and each member presented with a certain number of copies for distribution.

When does the Legislature elect a United States Senator? On the first Tuesday after the convening of the session next preceding the expiration of a Senatorial term.

How do they proceed? On the said Tuesday each House takes a separate vote for a United States Senator; on Wednesday (the day following) at 12 o'clock the Senate rises and proceeds to the Hall of the House of Representatives, and there in joint session they take a joint vote for a United States Senator; should there be an election it is so announced, but if not they must meet in joint session from day to day and take at least one ballot until an election is effected.

In joint sessions who is the presiding officer? The Speaker of the Senate, assisted by the Speaker of the House.

Who is clerk? The clerk of the Senate, assisted by the clerk of the House.

Which roll is called first? That of the Senate.

Where are the proceedings recorded? On the journals of each house.

Who is Sergeant-at-Arms? The Sergeant-at-Arms of the Senate, assisted by the one of the House.

CHAPTER IX.

LEGISLATION.

How many kinds of legislation are there? Two; exclusive and concurrent.

Name the things which are exclusive to the Senate? Confirming the Governor's appointments and trying impeachments.

What vote is necessary to confirm an appointment? A majority.

When trying impeachments shall the Senators be under oath? They shall.

What is necessary to a conviction? Two-thirds of the members present.

Who are liable to impeachment? The Governor and all civil officers.

To what shall conviction extend? To removal from office and disqualification to hold any office of honor, profit or trust in the State forever afterward.

Shall such a person be liable to indictment, trial and punishment by law? He shall.

Name the things exclusive to the House of Representatives? The sole power of impeachment and the origination of bills for raising revenue.

In considering bills for raising revenue what may the Senate do? Propose amendments as in other bills, provided they do not introduce any new matter under color of amendment which does not relate to revenue.

What are the powers of both Houses in concurrent legislation? They are co-ordinate or equal.

What is concurrent legislation? That in which both Houses take a part.

Enumerate the principal items of concurrent legislation? The election of a United States Senator, Librarian and Public Printer, and all bills, orders, and resolutions (except origination of bills for raising revenue).

How is every bill preceded? By a leave or permission.

What are leave-days? Days set apart for granting permissions or leaves to bring in bills.

When a bill is introduced what is done with it? It is referred to an appropriate committee.

What does the committee do with it? They consider and act upon it and refer it back to the House in which it originated with an expression of opinion that it ought or ought not to pass.

How must every bill be acted upon? It must have three several readings on three different days, unless the rule be suspended by a four-fifths vote, in which case it is put upon its passage immediately.

Should it pass that house what is done with it? It is sent to the other house to be acted upon in like manner.

Should it pass that House then where is it sent? To the Governor for his signature.

In case he signs it what is done with it? It is returned to the House in which it originated, enrolled, signed by the Speakers of both Houses, and becomes a law.

Should the Governor veto it what is done with it? He returns it to the House in which it originated together with his objections in writing, which are entered in full on the journal.

If a vetoed bill be reconsidered what vote is necessary to make it a law "over his head?" A majority of all the members of each House.

How shall this vote be taken? By the yeas and nays.

How else may a bill become a law without the Governor's signature? By default.

Give the way in which a bill may become a law by default? If the Governor should fail to return a bill within ten days (Sundays excepted) it becomes a law, unless the Legislature should adjourn in the meantime, in which case it shall be returned in three days after the meeting of the next Legislature, or it becomes a law anyhow.

State in brief the three ways by which a bill may become a law? With the Governor's signature, over his head, and by default.

How is all voting done in the Legislature and by the people? *Viva voce.*

How many are sufficient to call the yeas and nays? Two.

How may the seat of government be removed? By an act in which two-thirds of all the members elected to each House shall concur.

Under this Constitution what limit is there to the public debt? It shall not exceed $500,000, unless it be necessary to increase it to repel invasions, suppress insurrections, or prepare for defense against threatened hostilities.

What is the "Bill of Rights?" An enumeration of certain inalienable and inherent rights which our forefathers have held sacred for hundreds of years, and which have been incorporated into all of our Constitutions.

What is the imperative duty of every citizen? To familiarize himself with all of these rights.

Where are they found? In article the thirteenth of the Constitution.

CHAPTER X.

EXECUTIVE DEPARTMENT.

Governor and Lieutenant-Governor.

In what is the Supreme executive power of this commonwealth vested? In a Governor.

When and by whom is the Governor elected? On the first Monday in August every fourth year, by the people.

In what year is the Governor and other State officers except Treasurer elected? In every year divisible by four with three for a remainder.

When is he inaugurated? On the fifth Tuesday after his election.

Eligibility? He must be a citizen of the United States, thirty-five years of age, and a citizen of the State six years next preceding his election.

Is he eligible for the next term? He is not.

Who is ineligible to the office of Governor? A Congressman, an officer of the United States, or a minister of the gospel.

Salary of Governor? $5,000 per year and the use of the Governor's mansion ready furnished.

What of him as a military officer? He is commander-in-chief of the army and navy of this Commonwealth and of the militia, except when it is called into the service of the United States.

Can he command in the field personally? Only when advised to do so by the General Assembly.

What of his power to fill vacancies? He shall have power to fill vacancies that may occur by granting commissions, which shall expire when the vacancies shall have been filled according to the Constitution.

Has he power to remit fines and forfeitures, grant reprieves and pardons? He has, with some exceptions.

In what cases can he not pardon? In cases of impeachment.

In cases of treason how long shall he have power to grant reprieves? Until the end of the next session of the General Assembly.

Can he remit the fees of clerks, sheriffs, or attorneys in penal or criminal cases? He can not.

Has he power to call extra sessions of the Legislature? He has.

What of his power to adjourn the Legislature? In case the two Houses fail to agree on a time he may adjourn them to a time not exceeding four months.

What is the last injunction of the Constitution concerning him? He shall take care that the laws be faithfully executed.

Lieutenant-Governor.

When and how is he elected? At the same time and in the same manner as the Governor.

Do the voters cast a separate vote for Governor and Lieutenant-Governor? They do.

Eligibility? Same as for Governor.

What is he by virtue of his office? Speaker of the Senate.

In what case would he become Governor? In case the Governor should die, be absent from the State, removed from office, or unable to fill it.

Should the Lieutenant-Governor act as Governor what would the Senate do for a Speaker? Elect one from among their number.

In case of death or other inability of both Governor and Lieutenant-Governor, who would become the chief executive? The Speaker *pro tempore* of the Senate.

In case they had no Speaker *pro tem.* what would be done? The Secretary of State would convene the Senate and they would proceed to elect one.

Compensation of Lieutenant-Governor? As Speaker of the Senate he gets the same as the Speaker of the House of Representatives; as Governor, he gets Governor's salary pro rata for the time he serves.

By what are the salaries of Speakers regulated? By the Legislature from time to time, and is usually about $10 per day.

CHAPTER XI.

OTHER STATE OFFICERS.

How are the other State officers chosen? Some are elected and some are appointed by the Governor.

Name those elected by the people? Treasurer, Auditor, Attorney General, Register of Land Office, Superintendent of Public Instruction, and the members of the State Board of Equalization.

Name those which are appointed by the Governor? Secretary of State, Adjutant General, State Geologist, Commissioner of Agriculture, and Commissioner of Mines.

Name those elected by the General Assembly? State Librarian and Public Printer.

Secretary of State.

How is he appointed? By the Governor, with the consent of the Senate.

Term of office? Same as that of Governor, unless sooner removed.

Who appoints the Assistant Secretary of State? The Secretary of State with the assent of the Governor.

Are they under oath? They are.

Who is keeper of the great seal of this Commonwealth? The Secretary of State.

To what does he affix this seal? To all commissions given by the Governor, and to all public documents of importance.

What are his duties with regard to the papers of unfinished business of the Legislature? He shall carefully inspect the same and preserve such as he deems worthy, and these he shall file away in his office with a label stating to what session they relate.

What important exchange may he make with other States? The exchange of our statutes for those of other

States; also decisions of our Court of Appeals for decisions of the Supreme Court of the United States.

What does he preserve in his office? The books and records, deeds, maps, and papers belonging to his office, and is required to arrange the same in convenient order.

What may he purchase for the use of the Commonwealth? Such books as the law requires to be distributed.

Other duties? Such as may be required of him by law.

What is his salary? $1,500 per year, payable monthly out of the Treasury.

What are the duties of the Adjutant General? He has charge of the war department of the State, such as the militia, the State guard, the arsenal and all the arms and accoutrements of war.

How does he rank as a military officer? Next to the Governor.

His salary? $1,200 per year.

What are the duties of the State Geologist? He, with his two assistants, shall make complete surveys of the State to ascertain its geological and mineralogical resources and make complete analysis of all specimens obtained or sent to them, and to make out and publish a full report of all their research and its result.

Has this been of any value to the State? It has and has many times repaid the various appropriations made to maintain it.

For what purpose is the Commissioner of Agriculture appointed? To collect crop and stock reports, tabulate and publish the same; to collect and distribute valuable seeds, encourage the propagation of choice fruits, and in various other ways encourage this branch of industry.

Commissioner of Mines.

His duties? To see that all the mines in the State are properly worked, and to attend to the development of any new ones pointed out by the State Geologist.

CHAPTER XII.

How is the Treasurer chosen? Elected by the people. Term of office? Two years.

Eligibility? He must be a citizen of the United States, twenty-four years of age, and must have resided in the State two years next preceding his election.

When is he elected? On the first Monday in August in the odd years.

When shall he enter upon the duties of his office? On the first Monday in January next succeeding his election.

What is the extent of his bond? He shall execute a bond, to be approved by the Governor, for three hundred thousand dollars.

What are his duties? To keep accounts of all moneys received into and paid out of the public treasury, and to make out complete and comprehensive reports of same by the 10th of October each year.

Upon what shall he receive money into and pay it out of the treasury? Only upon a certificate or warrant from the Auditor.

What of this warrant? It shall specify that the law

under which it is claimed expressly directs that the money shall be paid out of the public treasury.

What is his salary? $2,400 per year.

Is he eligible to re-election? He is, as often as the people see proper to choose him.

Who is the Auditor? He is the book-keeper of the State.

Eligibility? He must be a citizen of the United States, twenty-four years of age, and two years next preceding his election a citizen of Kentucky.

When is he elected? At the same time as the Governor.

When does he enter upon the duties of his office? On the first Monday in January next succeeding his election or appointment.

The limit of his bond? $200,000, to be approved by the Governor.

His salary? $2,500.

How payable? Monthly at the treasury upon the requisition of the Governor.

What of his assistant? He shall have power to appoint one assistant whose salary shall be $2,000 per annum.

How much is allowed annually for the hire of other clerks? $8,000.

What of the assistant and other clerks? They are under oath and must give bond for the faithful discharge of their duty.

Duties of the Auditor? To keep a separate account of all taxes collected, so as to exhibit the amount collected under each law; to keep a correct list of all balances due by the Commonwealth to individuals and by individuals to the Commonwealth.

He shall keep an account of all claims of debt or credit which may exist between the General Government and this State, and between this State and any other State. He shall keep an account between the Commonwealth and all her civil officers whose salaries or wages are payable out of the treasury; the compensation to members of the General Assembly and the other officers thereof, and he shall audit and enter into account all other demands payable at the treasury, and all accounts of the collections of the revenue or other tax or public money, and of all public debts.

When does he make out and submit his biennial report to the Legislature? On or before the sixth day of each session.

What does this report exhibit? An account of all money paid into the treasury, by whom and for what account paid; the amount of public expenditures and each item thereof, and a vast amount of statistical and other valuable information collected by the assessors.

What is the duty of every citizen respecting this report? To procure it or an abstract of it, and to study it with great care and deep interest.

What is the Attorney General? He is the lawyer of the State.

When is he elected? At the same time as the Governor.

His duties? To give legal counsel to any and all executive or ministerial officers of the State, and to institute and prosecute all litigation to which the State is a party.

How is his advice given? In writing.

What other duties? To prepare drafts of contracts, obligations or other instruments of writing necessary for public use.

His salary? $500 per year and two per cent. of all judgments in favor of the Commonwealth.

When is the Register of the Land Office elected? Same time as the Governor, and holds office four years.

What is the amount of his bond? $10,000.

His duties? He has charge of the land office which contains the original patents and surveys of all lands in Kentucky, together with their history.

His salary? $2,000 per year.

CHAPTER XIII.

When is the Superintendent of Public Instruction elected? At the same time as the Governor, and shall hold office four years.

What accounts does he keep? Accounts of all the orders drawn or countersigned by him on the Auditor; of all the returns of settlements with and changes in the office of Superintendents.

His report? He shall make biennially a report of the condition, progress and prospects of the common schools; the amount and condition of the school fund; abstracts of the reports of the county superintendents; the practical workings of the public school system, together with suggestions as to any alterations it may require, and such other statistics, facts, and information as may be of interest.

What other duties? He shall ascertain and announce the pro rata share of the common school fund for each child, and also the amount for each county.

What of reports, registers, &c.? He shall prepare suitable blanks for reports, registers, certificates and notices, and distribute them to the superintendents of the different counties for the use of the superintendents, trustees and teachers.

What of the school laws? Each school district in the State is to be presented from time to time with a full copy of the common school laws.

What of his connection with the State Board of Education? He is by virtue of his office Chairman of the Board.

Who are the other members? The Attorney General, Secretary of State and two professional teachers chosen by them.

His salary? $3,000, with office fixtures, books, stationery, postage and fuel needed to carry on the work of the office.

Of what does the State Board of Equalization consist? Of one member from each congressional district and the Auditor.

How and when are the members elected? By the qualified voters at each Congressional election.

Their duty? To equalize the taxes throughout the State.

Where do they meet? At Frankfort.

Their compensation? $5.00 per day and mileage.

How is the State Librarian elected? Every two years by the General Assembly.

His duties? He has charge of the State library and is general supervisor and custodian of the Capitol and its grounds and buildings. He also furnishes fuel for this building and supplies all stationery.

His salary? $1,000 per annum.

How is the Public Printer and Binder chosen? Elected by the General Assembly.

What is his business? To print and bind, according to order, all matter required by law to be put before the public, such as journals of the two Houses, Governor's message, reports of the different State officials, public and private laws, all blanks for public officers and all proclamations of the Governor, &c., &c., amounting in the aggregate to many thousand volumes.

Compensation? It is one of the best offices in the State, as he is paid according to the amount of business done.

CHAPTER XIV.

JUDICIAL DEPARTMENT.

Courts:

In what is the judicial power of this Commonwealth vested? In such courts as are established by the Constitution and the General Assembly.

Name the courts established by the Constitution. Court of Appeals, Circuit Courts, County Courts, and Magisterial Courts.

Name those established by the General Assembly. Superior Court, Criminal Courts, Chancery Courts, and Common Pleas Courts.

COURT OF APPEALS.

What is the Supreme Court of Kentucky called? The Court of Appeals.

Its jurisdiction? It has only appellate jurisdiction.

Of what is it composed? Of four Appellate Judges, Clerk, Reporter, and Sergeant.

Into how many appellate districts is the State divided? Into four, beginning at the Eastern part of the State.

In what appellate district is this county? *See table of appellate districts.*

Which judge presides as Chief Justice? The one having the oldest commission or the shortest time to serve.

Term of office? Eight years.

How elected? By the people.

How are they classified? So that the term of office of one judge shall expire every two years.

Then how often does each district elect a judge? Once in every eight years.

Where is this court held? At Frankfort, and is in session every judicial day in the year, except during July and August, should business require it.

How many judges constitute a quorum to do business? Three.

Eligibility? He must be a citizen of the United States, thirty years of age, and two years next preceding his election a resident of the district from which he seeks to be elected, and the time served in the practice of law, or as judge, or both, must be equal to eight years.

Salary? $5,000 per year.

How are vacancies filled? By special election ordered by the Governor, unless the time be for less than one year, in which case it is filled by an appointment made by the Governor.

How is the Clerk of the Court of Appeals chosen? Elected by the people every eight years.

Eligibility? He must be a citizen of the United States, a resident of the State two years next preceding his election, and must have a certificate of qualification from an appellate or circuit judge.

His duties? To keep a record of the proceedings of the court.

Compensation? His fees, which are numerous and large, making it one of the best paying offices in the State.

How are vacancies filled? By special election, or by appointment, if the time be for less than one year.

How is the reporter chosen? Appointed by the court.

His duties? To publish such of the decisions of the court as are ordered by the court.

Compensation? He receives an annual salary paid out of the treasury.

How is the Sergeant chosen? By the court, for a term of four years.

His duties? He is sheriff of the Court of Appeals.

CHAPTER XV.

SUPERIOR COURT.

When was it established? April 22, 1882.

For what purpose? To give temporary relief to the Court of Appeals.

What is the rank of this Court? It is intermediate between the Circuit Court and the Court of Appeals.

Of how may judges is it composed? Three, one from each Superior Court district.

Term of office? Four years.

Eligibility? Same as Judge of Court of Appeals.

Salary? $3,600.

CIRCUIT COURTS.

Into how many Circuit Court or Judicial districts is Kentucky divided? Nineteen.

How many were established at the time of the adoption of the Constitution? Twelve.

How often could a new district be made? Every four years until the number reached sixteen.

When could they exceed this number? Not until the population reached a million and a half.

When was the seventeenth district established? In 1876.

In which judicial district is this county? *See table of judicial districts.*

How often is the Circuit Court required to be held in each county? At least twice each year.

Jurisdiction? It "has original jurisdiction of all matters both in law and equity within its county, of which jurisdiction is not by law exclusively delegated to some other tribunal, and has all power necessary to carry into effect the jurisdiction given."

Term of office of Circuit Judge, Commonwealth's Attorney and Circuit Clerk? Six years.

In what years are they elected? In the years divisable by six, with two for a remainder.

How are the Judge and Commonwealth's Attorney elected? By the voters of the entire district.

How is the Circuit Clerk of each county elected? By the voters of the county.

Eligibility of Circuit Judge? He must be a citizen of the United States, thirty years of age and two years next preceding his election a citizen of the district from which he is elected; he must also have been a practicing lawyer eight years, or the time engaged in practicing law and serving as judge must amount to eight years.

What are his powers and duties? He is a conservator of the peace, and his duties are to organize and preside over the court, to instruct the juries, to decide points of law, pass sentences, grant decrees, and to oversee and direct the whole proceedings of the court.

His salary? $3,000 per year, payable monthly out of the treasury.

How would a vacancy be filled? By special election.

Eligibility of the Commonwealth's Attorney? He must be a citizen of the United States, at least twenty-four years age, must have been a resident of the State two years and of the district one year next preceding his election, and a licensed practicing lawyer for two years.

What are his duties? To attend each Circuit Court held in his district, and to prosecute all violations of the criminal and penal laws therein, and to discharge all other duties assigned him by law.

His salary? $500 per year and thirty per cent. of all judgments rendered in favor of the Commonwealth in the several courts of his district.

Should a judgment be less than fifty dollars, what is his fee? Five dollars taxed as *cost*.

Eligibility of Circuit Clerk? He must be a citizen of the United States, twenty-one years of age, and must have a certificate of qualification from a circuit or an appellate judge.

His duties? To keep a record of all the orders and proceedings of the Circuit Court in his county, grant certificates to witnesses, to administer oaths, and perform such other duties as may by law be required of him by the Circuit Judge.

What is required before he can obtain the office? He must give bond for the faithful discharge of his duties.

His compensation? His fees.

How are vacancies filled? By appointment by the Circuit Judge.

Who is the ministerial officer of the Circuit Court? The sheriff of the county in which it is held.

CHAPTER XVI.

JURIES.

What of the right of trial by jury? It is very ancient and is esteemed one of our most sacred privileges.

How long has it been in vogue? Probably more than a thousand years.

How many kinds of juries are there? Two; Grand and Petit Juries.

How many constitute the Grand Jury? Sixteen.

Give the qualification of a grand juryman? He must be a white citizen, a housekeeper and over twenty-one years of age.

Who are incompetent to serve as Grand Jurors? All civil officers, surveyors of the public highway (road overseer), owners of grist-mills, venders of ardent spirits by license, chairman of school trustees, &c.,

Where does the Grand Jury sit? Apart from the court in a room to themselves.

Who presides over the Grand Jury? One of their number appointed by the judge as foreman.

In what kind of cases do they act? In criminal cases only.

What is their finding called? An indictment.

How many votes necessary to an indictment? Twelve.

Who draws up the indictment? The Commonwealth's Attorney.

What does the foreman write upon the indictment? The words "a true bill," and he also signs it as foreman.

To whom are these indictments reported and delivered? To the judge.

Compensation Grand Jurors? $1.50 per day.

Of how many jurors does the Petit Jury consist? Twelve.

How many are summoned to attend each court? Fifty-six.

Qualification of a petit juror? He must be a white citizen, at least twenty-one years of age, a housekeeper, sober, temperate, discreet, and of good demeanor.

In what kind of cases do they sit? In both criminal and civil cases.

Where does the petit jury sit? In the presence of the court and hears the testimony of the witnesses, the argument of the counsel, and the instruction of the judge, after which they retire to make up their decision.

What is this decision called? A verdict.

What of this verdict? If in a criminal case the verdict is "guilty" or "not guilty." If in a civil case it says how much one party, if any, is indebted to the other.

Compensation of petit jurors? $2.00 a day.

How are all jurors selected? By Jury Commissioners.

When? At the court next preceding the one in which they are to serve.

How many jury commissioners are appointed and how? Three men are appointed, sworn, and instructed by the Circuit Judge to act as commissioners.

How do they proceed in the selection of Grand Jurors? They retire to a private room and make up a list of at least thirty-two names of competent men from different parts of the county; these are written upon ballots and shaken together, and the first sixteen drawn out constitute the Grand Jury, and their names are written in a list, certified to, sealed and delivered to the judge.

How is the Petit Jury selected? The commissioners write the names of 100 men from different parts of the county on slips of paper and shake them together and draw out thirty ballots one by one, and these names form the list of petit jurors.

What is done with this list? It is certified to, sealed and endorsed "a list of the standing jury," and delivered to the judge together with a list of the remainder of the names not so drawn.

What does the judge do with these lists? He delivers them to the clerk in open court and swears him not to open them until the time prescribed by law; thirty days previous to the next term of court, and not before.

What does the clerk do at the proper time? Gives the lists to the sheriff, who summons the men.

How long before court must a juror be summoned? At least three days.

Should a grand juror fail to answer a summons what would be the penalty? A fine not exceeding ten dollars.

What the fine in case of a petit juror? From one to thirty dollars.

CHAPTER XVII.

COUNTY COURTS.

How often are county courts held? Once a month at the county seat.

Who are the officers of a county court? The county judge, county clerk, county attorney and sheriff.

Term of office of a county judge? Four years.

How chosen? By the people.

Eligibility? He must be a citizen of the United States, over twenty-one years of age, and a resident of the State two years, and of the county one year next preceding his election.

To whom does he execute a bond? To the circuit court clerk.

Is he a peace officer? He is, within his own county, and has all the powers of a justice of the peace in criminal and penal cases.

His duty as regards bonds of county officials? He is required to take and approve all bonds of county officers.

His power to appoint guardians, administrators, etc.? It is his duty to appoint them and make settlements with them.

Who has power to establish justices' districts and election precincts in a county? The county judge.

Who appoints the officers of elections? The county judge.

His duty relative to the Court of Claims? To call the court together and preside over it.

When and by whom are road surveyors and viewers appointed? By the county judge at a regular term of the county court.

When and by whom are orders to open, alter or discontinue roads made? At a regular county court by the county judge.

Where must application for tavern or drug license be made? At the county court.

Compensation of county judge? A yearly allowance out of the county levy, and his fees.

How are vacancies filled? By the Board of Magistrates.

County Clerk:

Term of office? Four years.

How chosen? By the people.

Qualification? He must be twenty-one years of age, two years a citizen of the State, and one year next preceding his election a citizen of the county.

His duty? To keep a record of all proceedings of the county court, to record deeds and mortgages, to issue marriage and other license, and to keep in his custody the bonds of the county officers, the assessors' books, poll books and other papers and documents required to be kept in his office.

Is he under bond? He is required to give bond with approved security before the county judge for the faithful discharge of his duties.

His compensation? His fees.

County Attorney:

Who is the County Attorney? He is the lawyer of the county.

Term of office? He is chosen by the voters for four years.

Eligibility? He must be twenty-one years of age, a citizen of the State two years, and of the county one year next preceding his election, and must have been a practicing lawyer two years.

His duties? To attend all county courts and courts of

claims, and defend and protect the interests of the county in said courts; to give such legal advice to county officers as may be required of him; to oppose the improper grant of tavern license; to oppose the wrongful alteration or discontinuance of any public road; to prosecute all criminal and penal offenses in his county, and to institute and conduct suits, etc., before any court in the State in which his county is interested when so directed by the county court.

Compensation? Thirty per cent. of the fines and forfeitures and an allowance out of the county levy.

CHAPTER XVIII.

Quarterly Courts:

Who holds the quarterly courts? The county judge.

When? In the months of January, April, July and October.

Who keeps the record in this court? The county judge himself.

In what do the quarterly courts have concurrent original jurisdiction with the circuit courts? In all actions for the recovery of money or personal property where the matter in controversy, exclusive of interest and costs, exceeds one hundred dollars and does not exceed two hundred dollars.

When would the quarterly court have concurrent original jurisdiction with the magistrate's court? When by consent of the defendants, in writing, or when one of them resides in the civil district which embraces the county seat, or when both of them are non-residents of the county.

State briefly the design of this court? To enable creditors to collect small amounts without delaying for the action of the circuit court.

Who constitute the Court of Claims? The Board of Magistrates together with the county judge.

Who presides over this court? The county judge.

For what purpose is this court held? To fix the county levy and make the necessary appropriations to meet the expenses of the county, such as salaries of county officials, appropriations for work done on the public roads, maintenance of paupers, &c.

Magistrates' Courts:

How is each county divided? Into a number of magisterial districts.

How many magistrates to each district? Two.

How often do they hold court? Each one holds a court every three months.

Jurisdiction in civil cases? $100.

Can juries be obtained in magistrates' courts? They can.

How? From among the by-standers.

How many form a magistrate's jury? Six.

What of the record in such courts? Each justice keeps his own record.

General duties of a magistrate? They are numerous and important, and our magistrates should be our wisest and best men; they compose the county levy court, have charge of the finances, are conservators of the peace, may issue warrants of arrest, hold examining trials, cite criminals to further trial, &c.

Compensation? Their fees; these are few and insignificant, and provision should be made for their better payment.

How are vacancies filled? By appointments made by the Governor.

Who is the ministerial officer of the magistrate's court? The constable.

What of his bond? He is required to give bond with approved security before the county court for the faithful discharge of his duty.

What processes may a constable execute? Bench warrants, warrants of arrest, distress or other warrants, summons, *subpœnas*, attachments of all kinds, notices, rules and orders of court in all criminal, penal and civil cases, and shall make due returns of same to the courts or persons issuing them.

Compensation? His fees.

Franklin Circuit Court:

What of the jurisdiction of this court? It shall have jurisdiction in behalf of the Commonwealth, of all causes, suits and motions against clerks of courts, collectors of public money, and all public debtors and defaulters of any denomination, and others claiming under them; and for this purpose its jurisdiction shall be coextensive with the State.

When does the judge of the Franklin Circuit Court hold a special term for the trial of actions and motions in favor of the Commonwealth? Beginning on the third Monday in June each year.

How long does it continue in session? Twelve days, or, if the business requires it, longer.

Could such cases be tried at a regular term of the Franklin Circuit Court? They could.

Special Courts:

Name the courts established by special acts of the Legislature? Court of common pleas, criminal courts, and chancery courts.

What is the object in establishing these courts? To facilitate litigation.

What courts do they closely resemble? The circuit courts.

What are the qualifications of the judges? Same as for circuit judge.

Salary? Generally same as circuit judge.

CHAPTER XIX.

OTHER COUNTY OFFICERS.

What other county officers besides county judge, clerk and attorney? Sheriff, assessor, jailer, superintendent common schools, surveyor and coroner.

When are sheriffs elected? On the first Monday in August in the even years.

Is he required to give bond? He is required to give a heavy bond.

When does he enter upon the duties of his office? On the first of January next following his election.

How many successive terms may a sheriff hold? Two; he is then ineligible for two years.

Enumerate his principal duties? To attend the circuit, county, and quarterly courts and court of claims held in his county, and keep order in them; to execute those condemned to be hung; to convey convicts to the penitentiary; to collect county and State taxes and pay same over to proper authority; to maintain the peace and make arrests; to execute all civil and criminal processes, notices, rules of court and similar papers placed in his hands.

What of deputies? He may appoint deputies having same power as himself.

Compensation? His fees.

Assessor:

How often is the assessor elected? Every four years.
How are his assistants chosen? By himself.
What are the duties of the assessor and his deputies? To list and fix a full and fair value on all the property in the county subject to taxation. He is also a kind of census officer and takes a list of the legal voters, the enrolled militia, children of school age, deaths, births, marriages, etc.

In case persons should fail or refuse to give a list to the assessor, what is his duty respecting such? To report them to the county clerk.

Compensation of assessor? A certain rate per cent on all lists.

Board of Supervisors:

Of whom is this board composed? Of three discreet taxpayers appointed by the county judge to revise the tax lists as reported by the assessor.

Jailer:

Term of office? Four years.

Duties? To receive and keep all persons placed in jail, and to furnish them with food and lodging and treat them humanely.

Should a person die in jail what is done with the corpse? It is delivered by the jailer to friends or buried decently by him at the expense of the county.

Besides keeping the jail what other duties has he? He is the janitor of the court house, and often acts as a ministerial officer to the courts.

Is he required to give bond? He is.

His compensation? His fees.

Superintendent Common Schools:

Term of office? Four years.

Eligibility? He must be a citizen of the United States, twenty-one years of age, two years a resident of the State, and one year next preceding his election a resident of the county, and he must have a certificate of qualification from the State Board of Examiners.

Is he required to give bond? He is.

His duties? To have general supervision over all the public schools in his county; to report to the State Superintendent the census of each school district in his county; to draw and collect the public money and pay the same to the teachers; to appoint two examiners; to grant certificates of qualification to teachers; to establish, change or abolish districts; to visit the schools; to condemn school houses; to make an annual report to the Superintendent of Public Instruction, and to make an annual settlement with the county judge. He is also required by law to procure suitable aid and hold, once a year, an institute for the benefit of the teachers of his county.

Are all teachers of public schools required by law to attend this Institute? They are.

His compensation? An annual allowance by the court of claims, to be paid out of the county levy.

County Surveyor:

When is he elected? Every four years.

Is he under bond? He is.

His duties? To make all surveys ordered by the court, and make out and return a plat and certificate of the same.

Compensation? His fees.

Coroner:

Term of office? Four years.

His duties? To hold inquests over bodies of persons murdered, drowned or otherwise killed suddenly, and ascertain, as nearly as possible, the exact cause and manner of the death of such persons.

How is this done? By a jury.

Of how many does the coroner's jury consist? Six men.

What is done with the body over which the inquest is held? It is delivered to friends or buried at the expense of the county.

What of his ministerial power? It is the same as that of the sheriff, and should the sheriff commit a crime the coroner has power to arrest him for trial.

Compensation? His fees.

How are vacancies in the offices of county clerk, county attorney, sheriff, jailer, assessor, superintendent of schools, surveyor and coroner filled? By appointments made by the county judge.

How long would such appointees serve? Till the next regular election.

CHAPTER XX.

CRIMES AND PUNISHMENTS.

What are crimes? Offenses against, or violations of, the law.

Into what two classes are crimes divided? Crimes are divided according to their enormity into felonies and misdemeanors.

What crimes are denominated felonies? Those punishable with death or confinement in the penitentiary.

What crimes are denominated misdemeanors? Those punishable by confinement in the county jail, or by fines.

Enumerate some of the principal felonies? Murder, treason, voluntary manslaughter, robbery and burglary, maiming, arson, perjury, grand larceny, embezzlement, forgery, counterfeiting, &c., &c.

What is the penalty for willful murder? Death or confinement in the penitentiary for life, in the discretion of the jury.

Penalty for treason? Death or confinement in the penitentiary, from ten to twenty years, at the discretion of the jury.

What is voluntary manslaughter? Killing a person in the heat of passion.

What is the penalty? Confinement from two to twenty-one years.

What is burglary? The unlawful breaking into a house.

What is the penalty for robbery and burglary? Confinement in the penitentiary from two to ten years.

What is maiming? Unlawfully putting out an eye, cutting, biting off or slitting the tongue, nose, ear or lip, or cutting or biting off any other limb or member of another person.

Penalty for maiming? Confinement from one to five years.

What is arson? The unlawful or malicious burning or firing of a building or other property.

Penalty? Confinement from five to twenty-one years, according to the nature of the case and the discretion of the jury.

What is perjury? False swearing.

Penalty? Confinement from one to five years, unless a different punishment is prescribed by law.

What is larceny? Stealing.

What two kinds of larceny? Grand and petit larceny.

What is grand larceny? The stealing of money or goods to the extent of ten dollars or over.

What is petit larceny? Theft of anything of less than ten dollars in value.

When was the amount distinguishing grand and petit larceny raised from four to ten dollars? In 1876.

Penalty for grand larceny? Confinement in the penitentiary from one to five years.

What is embezzlement? The fraudulently converting to one's own use the money or other effects of corporations or individuals with which he is entrusted.

Penalty? Confinement from one to ten years.

What is the punishment for counterfeiting? Confinement in the penitentiary from five to fifteen years.

For forgery? Confinement from two to fifteen years.

Enumerate some of the principal misdemeanors? Petit larceny, carrying concealed deadly weapons, breach of the peace, selling liquor without license, Sabbath-breaking, &c.

What is the penalty for misdemeanors? Imprisonment in county jail, or fines, or both.

CHAPTER XXI.

ELECTIONS AND ELECTION RETURNS.

What two general elections have we in Kentucky? The August election and the November election.

When is the August election held? On the first Monday in August.

When is the November election held? On the first Tuesday after the first Monday in November.

What officers are elected at the August election? All State, district and county officers, except the members of the State Board of Equalization.

What officers are chosen at the November election?

Electors for President and Vice-President, Congressmen and members of the State Board of Equalization.

How is each county divided? Into a number of election districts, each of which contains one or more voting places called *precincts.*

How are elections conducted at the polls or voting places? By election officers appointed for the purpose.

How many officers are appointed to act at each poll? Two judges and a clerk appointed by the county court, and a sheriff appointed by the county sheriff.

For how long are they appointed? For one year.

What is their compensation? Two dollars per day, and the sheriff gets in addition eight cents per mile for each mile of the distance from the precinct to the county seat traveled in delivering the poll books.

Between what hours must elections be held? Between 6 A. M. and 7 P. M.

Are the officers under oath? They are.

How is voting done? *Viva voce* except for Congressman, which is done by ballot.

Who compose the county board to examine the poll books? The county judge, county clerk and sheriff, or any two of them.

How soon after election days must the poll-books be returned to the county clerk? Within two days.

When are the poll-books compared? On the third day after the election, between the hours of ten and twelve o'clock.

In the election of county officers, and magistrates, and constables how many certificates are made out? Three.

What is done with them? One is delivered to the

party elected, another is sent to the Secretary of State, and the third is retained by the county clerk.

In the election of Representatives and State Senators how many certificates are made out? At least two.

What is done with these? One is retained in the clerk's office and one is given to the person elected, if the district is composed of but one county; but if the district is composed of more than one county, one certificate is retained by each county clerk and one given to the sheriff of each county.

Where two or more counties vote together for a Representative or Senator, who constitutes the Board of Examiners? The sheriffs of the different counties.

When do they meet to compare the vote? Between ten and twelve o'clock on the morning of the first Monday after the election?

Where? At the county clerk's office of the county first named in the district.

How many certificates of election do they make out and sign? Three.

What is done with them? One is retained in the said clerk's office, one is delivered to the person elected, and the third is sent to the Secretary of State.

In the election of all other officers how many certificates does each county board make out? Three.

What is done with these? One is retained in the clerk's office, one is sent by the clerk by mail, and another by private conveyance, to the Secretary of State at the seat of government.

Who constitutes the State board for examining the returns of elections? The Governor, Attorney General, Secretary of State, and in the absence of either, the Auditor and any two of them.

When does this State board meet? On the fourth Monday after the election.

How many certificates do they make out? Two, except for Congressman.

What is done with them? One is retained by the Secretary of State and the other is sent by mail to the person elected?

In election of Congressmen how many certificates are made out? Three.

What is done with these? One is retained by the Secretary of State, another is sent by mail to the person elected, and the third is sent by mail to the clerk of the last House of Representatives, at Washington, D. C.

What is the duty of the Secretary of State with regard to election returns? He shall publish the same in at least two newspapers of the State.

What of the certificate of the election of a United States Senator? It must be certified by the Governor under the seal of the State and countersigned by the Secretary of State, and then forwarded by mail to the President of the Senate, Washington, D. C.

Municipal Government.

CITY OF LOUISVILLE.

(The following is an outline of the government of Louisville which may be taken as a fair sample of city government in general.)

By what authority is city government established? That of the Legislature.

How many departments in the government of Louisville? It is similar to the general government, and has three departments, viz, Legislative, Executive, and Judicial.

In what is the Legislative power vested? In a Board of Common Councilmen and a Board of Aldermen, which together are styled "the General Council of the city of Louisville."

Eligibility of a Councilman? He must be a citizen of the United States, twenty-four years of age (an Alderman must be thirty years of age), and must have resided one year in the city of Louisville, and five years in the county of Jefferson next preceding his election, and he must be a *bona-fide* resident of the ward from which he is chosen.

Can he hold any other office or agency under the city, county, State, or United States Government, or any foreign government? He can not; neither must he be connected in any way with any corporation, contract, or enterprise, the emoluments of which are calculated to influence him as a member.

How are members chosen? By the qualified voters.

Into how many wards is the city divided? Twelve.

How many members are chosen from each ward? Two common Councilmen and one Alderman.

Term of office? Alderman two years, Councilman one year.

How are Aldermen divided? So that the term of office of one-half of them expires every year. (By this method each ward elects two Councilmen every year, and an Alderman every second year).

Do the two boards meet in the same room? They do not, but may hold joint sessions.

Exclusive privileges of each board? To judge of its own election returns, choose its own officers, appoint its own committees, keep its own journal, try and expel its own members, make its own standing rules, &c.

Officers of each board? President, Clerk, Sergeant-at-Arms and a Doorkeeper.

Duties of these officers? Such as are prescribed by law. (They are too numerous to be inserted here).

Powers and duties of the General Council? To make and enforce all ordinances necessary for the government and regulation of the city; such as to levy and apportion taxes, to create and maintain a police force, a fire department, a board of health; to furnish the city with water, light, and sewerage; to lay out, make and repair streets; to provide and maintain suitable public buildings for the various wants of the city, and to elect all municipal officers necessary to execute the ordinances relative to the general welfare of the city, except such as are, by law, chosen by the people at the general election for city officers.

In joint sessions who presides? The President of the Board of Aldermen.

How is voting done? *Viva voce.*

Where must all questions for raising revenue originate? In the Board of Common Councilmen.

EXECUTIVE DEPARTMENT.

In whom is the Executive power vested? In a Mayor.
Eligibility of Mayor? Same as for Alderman.
Term of office? Three years.

His duties and business? He is the head of the police force, and has power to direct and control them and to summon any number of citizens to act as special police, and if necessary he shall command in person; it is also his duty to give information, in writing, to the General Council of the condition of the affairs of the city, and to make suggestions concerning necessary legislation; to approve or disapprove all ordinances passed by General Council; to exercise a general supervision over all executive and ministerial officers of the city; to commission all officers, and to see that all the ordinances of the city are faithfully carried out.

Salary of Mayor? $5,000 per year.

JUDICIAL DEPARTMENT.

In what is the Judicial power vested? In the City Court of Louisville.

Officers of said court? Judge, Clerk, Marshal, Prosecuting Attorney, and Reporter.

Jurisdiction? It shall have original and exclusive jurisdiction over all unindictable misdemeanors committed within the city; it has power to arrest and hold examining trials of persons charged with felony; to try all complaints for breaches of the peace and city ordinances, and violations of the penal laws of the Commonwealth. The judge of said court is a general conservator of the peace within the city, and shall hold court every day except Sunday.

Districts.

SENATORIAL DISTRICTS OF KENTUCKY.

DISTRICTS.
- 7. Daviess, McLean.
- 8. Muhlenberg, Ohio, Butler.
- 10. Breckinridge, Hancock, Edmonson, Grayson.
- 12. Hardin, Meade, Bullitt.
- 13. Hart, Larue, Greene.
- 14. Spencer, Nelson, Shelby.
- 15. Marion, Washington, Taylor.
- 16. Clinton, Cumberland, Adair, Russell, Wayne.
- 18. Lincoln, Boyd, Garrard, Casey.
- 20. Anderson, Franklin, Mercer.
- 21. Henry, Oldham, Trimble, Carroll.
- 23. Gallatin, Boone, Owen.
- 24. Kenton.
- 25. Campbell.
- 27. Fayette.
- 28. Bourbon, Clark, Montgomery.
- 29. Madison, Estill, Rockcastle.
- 31. Mason, Lewis.
- 32. Boyd, Greenup, Lawrence, Elliott.

The above districts elect Senators in the years divisible by four with one remainder.

OF KENTUCKY.

SENATORIAL DISTRICTS—Continued.

DISTRICTS.
1. Hickman, Fulton, Graves.
2. McCracken, Ballard, Marshall.
3. Lyon, Livingston, Calloway, Trigg.
4. Caldwell, Crittenden, Webster.
5. Henderson, Union.
6. Christian, Hopkins.
9. Logan, Simpson, Todd.
11. Warren, Allen.
17. Laurel, Pulaski, Whitley, Bell, Knox, Jackson.
19. Barren, Metcalfe, Monroe.
22. Woodford, Scott, Jessamine.
26. Bracken, Pendleton, Grant.
30. Nicholas, Harrison, Robertson.
33. Perry, Letcher, Clay, Harlan, Floyd, Pike, Martin.
34. Magoffin, Breathitt, Johnson, Menifee, Morgan, Wolf, Owsley, Powell, Lee.
35. Rowan, Bath, Fleming, Carter.
36. Jefferson county and 1st and 2ond wards of Louisville.
37. 3rd, 4th, 5th, 6th, and 7th wards of Louisville.
38. 8th, 9th, 10th, 11th, and 12th wards of Louisville.

The above districts elect Senators in the years divisible by four with three remainder.

APPELLATE DISTRICTS OF KENTUCKY.
FIRST DISTRICT.

Bath, Bell, Boyd, Bracken, Breathitt, Bourbon, Carter, Clark, Clay, Elliott, Estill, Fleming, Floyd, Greenup, Harlan, Johnson, Jackson, Knott, Knox, Laurel, Leslie, Letcher, Lee, Lewis, Lawrence, Madison, Montgomery, Mason, Morgan, Magoffin, Martin, Menifee, Nicholas, Owsley, Powell, Perry, Pike, Robertson, Rockcastle, Rowan, Wolf.

SECOND DISTRICT.

Anderson, Boone, Boyle, Campbell, Carroll, Casey, Clinton, Fayette, Franklin, Gallatin, Garrard, Grant, Harrison, Henry, Jessamine, Kenton, Lincoln, Mercer, Owen, Pendleton, Pulaski, Russell, Scott, Trimble, Wayne, Whitley, Woodford.

THIRD DISTRICT.

Adair, Allen, Barren, Breckinridge, Bullitt, Cumberland, Green, Hardin, Hart, Jefferson, Larue, Marion, Meade, Metcalfe, Monroe, Nelson, Oldham, Shelby, Spencer, Taylor, Washington.

FOURTH DISTRICT.

Ballard, Butler, Caldwell, Calloway, Carlisle, Christian, Crittenden, Daviess, Edmonson, Fulton, Grayson, Graves, Hancock, Henderson, Hickman, Hopkins, Livingston, Logan, Lyon, Marshall, McCracken, McLean, Muhlenberg, Ohio, Simpson, Trigg, Todd, Union, Warren, Webster.

CIRCUIT COURT OR JUDICIAL DISTRICTS.

First District.—Ballard, Calloway, Carlisle, Fulton, Graves, Hickman, Livingston, Marshall, McCracken.

Second District.—Caldwell, Christian, Hopkins, Lyon, Muhlenberg, Trigg.

Third District.—Crittenden, Henderson, Union, Webster.

Fourth District.—Daviess, Hancock, McLean, Ohio.

Fifth District.—Butler, Logan, Simpson, Todd, Warren.

Sixth District.—Breckinridge, Edmonson, Grayson, Hardin, Meade.

Seventh District.—Adair, Allen, Barren, Clinton, Cumberland, Green, Hart, Metcalfe, Monroe.

Eighth District.—Boyle, Casey, Garrard, Lincoln, Pulaski, Rockcastle, Russell, Wayne.

Ninth District.—Jefferson.

Tenth District.—Bourbon, Clark, Fayette, Jessamine, Madison, Scott, Woodford.

Eleventh District.—Boone, Carroll, Franklin, Gallatin, Grant, Owen.

Twelfth District,—Bracken, Campbell, Harrison, Kenton, Pendleton, Robertson.

Thirteenth District.—Bath, Elliott, Magoffin, Menifee, Montgomery, Morgan.

Fourteenth District.—Fleming, Greenup, Lewis, Mason, Nicholas, Rowan.

Fifteenth District.—Bell, Harlan, Jackson, Knox, Laurel, Leslie, Owsley, Whitley.

Sixteenth District.—Boyd, Carter, Floyd, Johnson, Lawrence, Martin, Pike.

Seventeenth District.—Anderson, Bullitt, Henry, Oldham, Shelby, Spencer, Trimble.

Eighteenth District.—Larue, Marion, Mercer, Nelson, Taylor, Washington.

Nineteenth District.—Breathitt, Clay, Estill, Knott, Lee, Letcher, Perry, Powell, Wolf.

CONGRESSIONAL DISTRICTS OF KENTUCKY.

First District.—Composed of the counties of Ballard, Caldwell, Carlisle, Calloway, Crittenden, Fulton, Graves, Hickman, Livingston, Lyon, McCracken, Marshall and Trigg.

Second District.—Counties of Christian, Daviess, Hancock, Henderson, Hopkins, McLean, Union and Webster.

Third District.—Counties of Allen, Butler, Clinton, Cumberland, Edmonson, Logan, Monroe, Muhlenberg, Simpson, Todd and Warren.

Fourth District.—Counties of Breckinridge, Bullitt, Grayson, Hardin, Larue, Marion, Meade, Nelson, Ohio and Washington.

Fifth District.—County of Jefferson.

Sixth District.—Counties of Boone, Campbell, Carroll, Gallatin, Grant, Kenton, Pendleton and Trimble.

Seventh District.—Counties of Bourbon, Fayette, Franklin, Harrison, Henry, Oldham, Owen, Scott and Woodford.

Eighth District.—Counties of Anderson, Boyle, Garrard, Jackson, Jessamine, Laurel, Lincoln, Madison, Mercer, Owsley, Rockcastle, Shelby and Spencer.

Ninth District.—Counties of Bath, Boyd, Bracken, Carter, Fleming, Greenup, Johnson, Lawrence, Lewis, Martin, Mason, Nicholas, Robertson and Rowan.

Tenth District.—Counties of Bell, Breathitt, Clark,

Clay, Elliott, Estill, Floyd, Harlan, Knott, Knox, Lee, Leslie, Letcher, Magoffin, Menifee, Montgomery, Morgan, Perry, Pike, Powell and Wolf.

Eleventh District.—Counties of Adair, Barren, Casey, Green, Hart, Metcalfe, Pulaski, Russell, Taylor, Wayne and Whitley.

Constitution

OF THE

STATE OF KENTUCKY.

PREAMBLE.

We, the representatives of the people of the State of Kentucky, in Convention assembled, to secure to all the citizens thereof the enjoyment of the rights of life, liberty, and property and of pursuing happiness, do ordain and establish this Constitution for its government.

ARTICLE FIRST.

Concerning the Distribution of the Powers of Government.

SECTION 1. The powers of the Government of the State of Kentucky shall be divided into three distinct departments, and each of them be confided to a separate body of magistracy, to-wit: those which are Legislative to one; those which are Executive to another; and those which are Judiciary to another.

SEC. 2. No person or collection of persons, being of one of those departments shall exercise any power properly belonging to either of the others, except in the instances hereinafter expressly directed or permitted.

ARTICLE SECOND.

Concerning the Legislative Department.

SECTION 1. The Legislative power shall be vested in a House of Representatives and Senate, which, together, shall be styled the General Assembly of the Commonwealth of Kentucky.

SEC. 2. The members of the House of Representatives shall continue in service for the term of two years from the day of the general election, and no longer.

SEC. 3. Representatives shall be chosen on the first Monday in August, in every second year; and the mode of holding the elections shall be regulated by law.

SEC 4. No person shall be a Representative, who at the time of his election, is not a citizen of the United States, has not attained the age of twenty-four years, and who has not resided in this State two years next preceding his election and the last year thereof in the county, town or city for which he may be chosen.

SEC. 5. The General Assembly shall divide each county in this Commonwealth into convenient election precincts, or may delegate power to do so to such county authorities as may be designated by law; and elections for Representatives for the several counties shall be held at their respective courts, and in the several election precincts into which the counties may be divided: *Provided*, That when it shall appear to the General Assembly that any city or town hath a number of qualified voters equal to the ratio then fixed, such city or town shall be invested with the privilege of a separate representation, in either or both houses of the General Assembly, which shall be retained so long as such city or town shall contain a number of qualified voters equal to the ratio which may from time to be fixed by law; and thereafter, elections for the county in which said city or town is situated shall not be held therein; but such city or town shall not be entitled to a separate representation unless such county, after the separation, shall also be entitled to one or more representatives. That whenever a city or town shall be entitled to a separate representation in either house of the General Assembly, and by its numbers shall be entitled to more than one Representative, such city or town shall be divided by squares which are contiguous, so as to make the most compact form, into Representative Districts, as nearly equal as may be, equal to the number of Representatives to which said city or town shall be entitled; and one Representative shall be elected from each district. In like manner shall said city or town be divided into Senatorial Districts, when, by the apportionment, more than one Senator shall be allotted to such city or town ; and a Senator shall be elected from each Senatorial District ; but no ward or municipal division shall be divided by such division of Senatorial or Representative Districts, unless it be necessary to equalize the Elective, Senatorial or Representative Districts.

SEC. 6. Representation shall be equal and uniform in this Commonwealth, and shall be forever regulated and ascertained by the number of qualified voters therein. In the year 1850, again in the year 1857, and every eighth year thereafter, an enumeration of all the qualified voters of the State shall be made; and to secure uniformity and equality of representation the State is laid off into ten districts. The first district shall be composed of the the counties of Fulton, Hickman, Ballard, McCraken, Graves, Calloway, Marshall, Livingston, Crittenden, Union, Hopkins, Caldwell and Trigg. The second district shall be composed of the counties of Christian, Muhlenberg, Henderson, Daviess, Hancock, Ohio, Breckinridge, Meade, Grayson, Butler and Edmonson. The third district shall be composed of the counties of Todd, Logan, Simpson, Warren, Allen, Monroe, Barren and Hart. The fourth district shall be composed of the counties of Cumberland, Adair, Green, Taylor, Clinton, Russell, Wayne. Pulaski, Casey, Boyle and Lincoln. The fifth district shall be composed of the counties of Hardin, Larue, Bullitt, Spencer, Nelson, Washington, Marion, Mercer and Anderson. The Sixth district shall be composed of the counties of Garrard, Madison, Estill, Owsley, Rockcastle, Laurel, Clay, Whitley, Knox, Harlan, Perry, Letcher, Pike, Floyd and Johnson. The Seventh district shall be composed of the counties of Jefferson, Oldham, Trimble, Carroll, Henry and Shelby and the city of Louisville. The eighth district shall be composed of the counties of Bourbon, Fayette, Scott, Owen, Franklin, Woodford, and Jessamine. The ninth district shall be composed of the counties of Clark, Bath, Montgomery, Fleming, Lewis, Greenup, Carter, Lawrence, Morgan, and Breathitt. The tenth district shall be composed of the counties of Mason, Bracken, Nicholas, Harrison, Pendleton, Campbell, Grant, Kenton, Boone, and Gallatin. The number of Representatives shall, at the several sessions of the General Assembly next after the making of the enumerations, be apportioned among the ten several districts, according to the number of qualified voters in each; and the Representatives shall be apportioned, as near as may be, among the counties, towns, and cities in each district; and in making such apportionment the following shall govern, to-wit: Every county, town, or city having the ratio shall have one Representative; if double the ratio, two Representatives, and so on. Next, the counties, towns, or cities, having one or more Representatives, and the largest number of qualified voters above the ratio, and counties having the largest number under the ratio, shall have a Representative, regard being always had to the greatest number of qualified voters: *Provided*, That when a county may not have a sufficient number of qualified voters to entitle it to one Representative, then such county may be joined to some adjacent county or counties, which counties shall send one Representative. When a a new county shall be formed of territory belonging to more than one district, it shall form a part of that district having the least number of qualified voters.

SEC. 7. The House of Representatives shall choose its Speaker and other officers.

SEC. 8. Every free white male citizen of the age of twenty-one years, who has resided in the State two years, or in the county, town, or city in which he offers to vote, one year next preceding the election, shall be a voter; but such voter shall have been, for sixty days next preceding the election, a resident of the precinct in which he offers to vote, and he shall vote in said precinct, and not elsewhere.

SEC. 9. Voters in all cases except treason, felony, breach or surety of the peace, shall be privileged from arrest during their attendance at, going to, and returning from elections.

SEC. 10. Senators shall be chosen for the term of four years, and the Senate shall have power to choose its officers biennially.

SEC. 11. Senators and Representatives shall be elected under the first apportionment after the adoption of this Constitution, in the year 1851.

SEC. 12. At the session of the General Assembly next after the first apportionment under this Constitution, the Senators shall be divided by lot, as equally as may be, into two classes; the seats of the first class shall be vacated at the end of two years from the day of the election, and those of the second class at the end of four years, so that one-half shall be chosen every two years.

SEC. 13. The number of Representatives shall be one hundred, and the number of Senators thirty-eight.

SEC. 14. At every apportionment of representation the State shall be laid off into thirty-eight Senatorial Districts, which shall be so formed as to contain, as near as may be, an equal number of qualified voters, and so that no county shall be divided in the formation of a Senatorial District, except such county shall be entitled, under the enumeration, to two or more Senators; and where two or more counties compose a district, they shall be adjoining.

SEC. 15. One Senator for each district shall be elected by the qualified voters therein, who shall vote in the precincts where they reside, at the places where elections by law are directed to be held.

SEC. 16. No person shall be a Senator who, at the time of his election, is not a citizen of the United States, has not attained the age of thirty years, and who has not resided in this State six years next preceeding his election, and the last year thereof in the district for which he may be chosen.

SEC. 17. The election of Senators next after the first apportionment under this Constitution, shall be general throughout the State, and at the same time that the election for Representatives is held, and thereafter there shall be a biennial election for Senators to fill the places of those whose term of service may have expired.

SEC. 18. The General Assembly shall convene on the first Monday in November after the adoption of this Constitution, and again on the first Monday in November, 1851, and on the same day of every second year thereafter, unless a different day be appointed by law, and their sessions shall be held at the seat of government.

SEC. 19. Not less than a majority of the members of each house of the General Assembly shall constitute a quorum to do business; but a smaller number may adjourn from day to day, and shall be authorized by law to compel the attendance of absent members in such manner and under such penalties as may be prescribed thereby.

SEC. 20. Each house of the General Assembly shall judge of the qualifications, elections, and returns of its members; but a contested election shall be determined in such manner as shall be directed by law.

SEC. 21. Each house of the General Assembly may determine the rules of its proceedings, punish a member for disorderly behavior, and, with the concurrence of two-thirds, expel a member; but not a second time for the same cause.

SEC. 22. Each house of the General Assembly shall keep and publish, weekly, a journal of its proceedings; and the yeas and nays of the members on any question shall, at the desire of any two of them, be entered on the journal.

SEC. 23. Neither house, during the session of the General Assembly, shall, without the consent of the other, adjourn for more than three days, nor to any other place than that in which they may be sitting.

SEC. 24. The members of the General Assembly shall severally receive from the public treasury a compensation for their services, which shall be three dollars a day during their attendance on, and twelve and a half cents per mile for the necessary travel in going to, and returning from, the sessions to their respective houses: *Provided*, That the same may be increased or diminished by law; but no alteration shall take effect during the session at which such alteration shall be made; nor shall a session of the General Assembly continue beyond sixty days, except by a vote of two-thirds of all the members elected to each house; but this shall not apply to the first session held under this Constitution.

SEC. 25. The members of the General Assembly shall, in all cases except treason, felony, breach or surety of the peace, be privileged from arrest during their attendance at the sessions of their respective houses, and in going to, and returning from, the same; and for any speech or debate in either house they shall not be questioned in any other place.

SEC. 26. No Senator or Representative shall, during the term for which he was elected, nor for one year thereafter, be appointed or elected to any civil office of profit under this Commonwealth, which shall have been erected, or the emoluments of which shall have been increased, during the said term, except to such offices or appointments as may be filled by the election of the people.

SEC. 27. No person, while he continues to exercise the functions of a clergyman, priest, or teacher of any religious persuasion, society, or sect, nor while he holds or exercises any office of profit under this Commonwealth, or under the Government of the United States, shall be eligible to the General Assembly, except attorneys at law, justices of the peace, and militia officers: *Provided*, That attorneys for the Commonwealth, who receive a fixed annual salary, shall be ineligible.

SEC. 28, No person who, at any time, may have been a collector of taxes or public moneys for the State, or the assistant or deputy of such collector, shall be eligible to the General Assembly, unless he shall have obtained a quietus six months before the election, for the amount of such collection, and for all public moneys for which he may have been responsible.

SEC. 29. No bill shall have the force of a law until, on three several days, it be read over in each house of the General Assembly, and free discussion allowed thereon, unless, in cases of urgency, four-fifths of the house where the bill shall be depending, may deem it expedient to dispense with this rule.

SEC. 30. All bills for raising revenue shall originate in the House of Representatives; but the Senate may propose amendments, as in other bills: *Provided*, That they shall not introduce any new matter, under color of amendment, which does not relate to raising revenue.

SEC. 31. The General Assembly shall regulate, by law, by whom and in what manner writs of election shall be issued to fill the vacancies which may happen in either branch thereof.

SEC. 32. The General Assembly shall have no power to grant divorces, to change the names of individuals, or direct the sales of estates belonging to infants, or other persons laboring under legal disabilities, by special legislation; but by general laws shall confer such powers on the courts of justice.

SEC. 33. The credit of this Commonwealth shall never be given or loaned in aid of any person, association, municipality, or corporation.

SEC. 34. The General Assembly shall have no power to pass laws to diminish the resources of the Sinking Fund, as now established by law, until the debt of the State be paid, but may pass laws to increase them; and the whole resources of said fund, from year to year, shall be sacredly set apart and applied to the payment of the interest and principal of the State debt, and to no other use or purpose, until the whole debt of the State is fully paid and satisfied.

SEC. 35. The General Assembly may contract debts to meet causal deficits or failures in the revenue; but such debts, direct or contingent. singly or in the aggregate, shall not at any time exceed five hundred thousand dollars; and the moneys arising from loans creating such debts shall be applied to the purpose for which they were obtained, or to repay such debts: *Provided*, That the State may contract debts to repel invasion, suppress insurrection, or, if hostilities are threatened, provide for the public defense.

SEC. 36. No act of the General Assembly shall authorize any debt to be contracted on behalf of the Commonwealth, except for the purposes mentioned in the thirty-fifth section of this article, unless provision be made therein to lay and collect an annual tax sufficient to pay the interest stipulated, and to discharge the debt within thirty years; nor shall such acts take effect until it shall have been submitted to the people at a general election, and shall have received a majority of all the votes cast for and against it: *Provided*, That the General Assembly may contract debts, by borrowing money to pay any part of the debt of the State, without submission to the people, and without making provision in the act authorizing the same for a tax to discharge the debt so contracted, or the interest thereon.

SEC. 37. No law enacted by the General Assembly shall relate to more than one subject, and that shall be expressed in the title.

SEC. 38. The General Assembly shall not change any venue

or any penal or criminal prosecution, but shall provide for the same by general laws.

SEC. 39. The General Assembly may pass laws authorizing writs of error in criminal or penal cases, and regulating the right of challenge of jurors therein.

SEC. 40. The General Assembly shall have no power to pass any act or resolution, for the appropriation of any money, or the creation of any debt, exceeding the sum of one hundred dollars, at any one time, unless the same, on its final passage, shall be voted for by a majority of all the members then elected to each branch of the General Assembly, and the yeas and nays thereon entered on the journal.

ARTICLE THIRD.
Concerning the Executive Department.

SEC. 1 The Supreme Executive power of the Commonwealth shall be vested in a Chief Magistrate, who shall be styled the Governor of the Commonwealth of Kentucky.

SEC. 2. The Governor shall be elected for the term of four years, by the qualified voters of the State, at the time when, and places where, they shall respectively vote for Representatives The person having the highest number of votes shall be Governor; but if two or more shall be equal and highest in votes, the election shall be determined by lot in such manner as the General Assembly may direct.

SEC. 3. The Governor shall be ineligible for the succeeding four years after the expiration of the term for which he shall have been elected.

SEC. 4. He shall be at least thirty-five years of age, and a citizen of the United States, and have been an inhabitant of this State at least six years next preceding his election.

SEC. 5. He shall commence the execution of the duties of his office on the fifth Tuesday succeeding the day of the general election on which he shall have been chosen, and shall continue in the execution thereof until his successor shall have taken the oaths or affirmations prescribed by this Constitution.

SEC. 6. No member of Congress, or person holding any office under the United States, or minister of any religious society, shall be eligible to the office of Governor.

SEC. 7. The Governor shall, at stated times, receive for his services a compensation, which shall neither be increased or diminished during the term for which he was elected.

SEC. 8. He shall be commander-in-chief of the army and navy of this Commonwealth, and of the militia thereof, except when they shall be called into the service of the United States; but he shall not command personally in the field, unless advised so to do by a resolution of the General Assembly.

SEC. 9. He shall have power to fill vacancies that may occur, by granting commissions, which shall expire when such vacancies shall have been filled according to the provisions of this Constitution.

SEC. 10. He shall have power to remit fines and forfeitures, grant reprieves and pardons, except in case of impeachment. In cases of treason, he shall have power to grant reprieves, until the end of the next session of the General Assembly, in which the power of pardoning shall be vested; but he shall have no power to remit the fees of the Clerk, Sheriff, or Commonwealth's Attorney, in penal or criminal cases.

SEC. 11. He may require information, in writing, from the officers in the executive department, upon any subject relating to the duties of their respective offices.

SEC. 12. He shall, from time to time, give to the General Assembly information of the state of the Commonwealth, and recommend to their consideration such measures as he may deem expedient.

SEC. 13. He may, on extraordinary occasions, convene the General Assembly at the seat of government, or at a different place if that should have become, since their last adjournment, dangerous from an enemy, or from contagious disorders; and in case of disagreement between the two houses, with respect to the time of adjournment, he may adjourn them to such time as he shall think proper, not exceeding four months.

SEC. 14. He shall take care that the laws be faithfully executed.

SEC. 15. A Lieutenant Governor shall be chosen at every regular election for Governor, in the same manner, to continue in office for the same time, and possessing the same qualifications as the Governor. In voting for Governor and Lieutenant Governor, the electors shall state for whom they vote as Governor, and for whom as Lieutenant Governor.

SEC. 16. He shall, by virtue of his office, be Speaker of the Senate, have a right, when in committee of the whole, to debate and vote on all subjects, and when the Senate are equally divided to give the casting vote.

SEC. 17. Should the Governor be impeached, removed from office, die, refuse to qualify, resign, or be absent from the State, the Lieutenant Governor shall exercise all the power and authority appertaining to the office of Governor, until another be duly elected and qualified, or the Governor, absent or impeached, shall return or be aquitted.

SEC. 18. Whenever the government shall be administered by the Lieutenant Governor, or he shall fail to attend as Speaker of the Senate, the Senators shall elect one of their own members as Speaker for that occasion And if, during the vacancy of the office of Governor, the Lieutenant Governor shall be impeached, removed from office, refuse to qualify, resign, die, or be absent from the State, the Speaker of the Senate shall, in like manner, administer the government: *Provided*, That whenever a vacancy shall occur in the office of Governor, before the first two years of the term shall have expired, a new election for Governor shall take place to fill such vacancy.

SEC. 19. The Lieutenant Governor, or Speaker *pro tempore*

of the Senate, while he acts as Speaker of the Senate, shall receive for his services the same compensation which shall, for the same period, be allowed to the Speaker of the House of Representatives, and no more; and during the time he administers the government as Governor, shall receive the same compensation which the Governor would have received had he been employed in the duties of his office.

Sec. 20. If the Lieutenant Governor shall be called upon to administer the Government, and shall, while in such administration, resign, die, or be absent from the State during the recess of the General Assembly, it shall be the duty of the Secretary of State, for the time being, to convene the Senate for the purpose of choosing a Speaker.

Sec. 21. The Governor shall nominate, and, by and with the advice and consent of the Senate, appoint a Secretary of State, who shall be commissioned during the term for which the Governor was elected, if he shall so long behave himself well. He shall keep a fair register, and attest all the official acts of the Governor, and shall, when required, lay the same and all papers, minutes, and vouchers, relative thereto, before either house of the General Assembly; and shall perform such other duties as may be required of him by law.

Sec. 22. Every bill which shall have passed both houses, shall be presented to the Governor. If he approve he shall sign it; but if not, he shall return it, with his objections, to the house in which it originated, who shall enter the objections at large upon their journal, and proceed to reconsider it. If, after such reconsideration, a majority of all the members elected to that house, shall agree to pass the bill, it shall be sent, with the objections, to the other house, by which it shall likewise be considered, and if approved by a majority of all the members elected to that house, it shall be a law; but in such cases the votes of both houses shall be determined by yeas and nays, and the names of the members voting for and against the bill shall be entered upon the journals of each house, respectively. If any bill shall not be returned by the Governor within ten days (Sundays excepted) after it shall have been presented to him, it shall be a law, in like manner as if he had signed it, unless the General Assembly, by their adjournment, prevent its return; in which case it shall be a law, unless sent back within three days after their next meeting.

SEC. 23. Every order, resolution, or vote, in which the concurrence of both houses may be necessary, except on a question of adjournment, shall be presented to the Governor, and, before it shall take effect, be approved by him; or, being disapproved, shall be re-passed by a majority of all the members elected to both houses, according to the rules and limitations prescribed in case of a bill.

SEC. 24. Contested elections for Governor and Lieutenant-Governor shall be determined by both houses of the General Assembly, according to such regulations as may be established by law.

SEC. 25. A Treasurer shall be elected by the qualified voters of the State, for the term of two years, and an Auditor of Public Accounts, Register of the Land Office, and Attorney General, for the term of four years. The duties and responsibilities of these officers shall be prescribed by law: *Provided*, That inferior State officers, not specially provided for in this Constitution, may be appointed or elected in such manner as shall be prescribed by law, for a term not exceeding four years.

SEC. 26. The first election under this Constitution for Governor, Lieutenant Governor, Treasurer. Auditor of Public Accounts, Register of the Land Office, and Attorney General, shall be held on the first Monday in August, in the year 1851.

ARTICLE FOURTH.
Concerning the Judicial Department.

SEC. 1. The judicial power of this Commonwealth, both as to matters of law and equity, shall be vested in one Supreme

Court (to be styled the Court of Appeals), the Courts established by this Constitution, and such Courts inferior to the Supreme Court, as the General Assembly may, from time to time, erect and establish.

Concerning the Court of Appeals.

SEC. 2. The Court of Appeals shall have appellate jurisdiction only, which shall be co-extensive with the State, under such restrictions and regulations, not repugnant to this Constitution, as may, from time to time, be prescribed by law.

SEC. 3. The Judges of the Court of Appeals shall, after their first term, hold their offices for eight years from and after their election, and until their successors shall be duly qualified, subject to the conditions hereinafter prescribed; but for any reasonable cause the Governor shall remove any of them, on the address of two-thirds of each house of the General Assembly: *Provided, however,* That the cause or causes for which such removals may be required, shall be stated at length in such address, and on the journal of each house. They shall, at stated times, receive for their services an adequate compensation, to be fixed by law, which shall not be diminished during the time for which they shall have been elected.

SEC. 4. The Court of Appeals shall consist of four Judges, any three of whom may constitute a Court for the transaction of business. The General Assembly, at its first session after the adoption of this Constitution, shall divide the State by counties into four districts, as nearly equal in voting population, and with as convenient limits as may be, in each of which the qualified voters shall elect one Judge of the Court of Appeals: *Provided,* That whenever a vacancy shall occur in said Court, from any cause, the General Assembly shall have power to reduce the number of Judges and districts; but in no event shall there be less than three Judges and districts. Should a change in the number of the Judges of the Court of Appeals be made, the term of office and number of districts shall be so changed as to preserve the principle of electing one Judge every two years.

SEC. 5. The Judges shall, by virtue of their offices, be conservators of the peace throughout the State. The style of all processes shall be, "The Commonwealth of Kentucky." All prosecutions shall be carried on in the name and by the authority of the Commonwealth of Kentucky, and conclude, "against the peace and dignity of the same."

SEC. 6. The Judges first elected shall serve as follows, to-wit: One shall serve until the first Monday in August, 1852; one until the first Monday in August, 1854; one until the first Monday in August, 1856; and one until the first Monday in August, 1858. The Judges, at the first term of the Court succeeding their election shall determine, by lot, the length of time which each one shall serve; and at the expiration of the service of each, an election in the proper district shall take place to fill the vacancy. The Judge having the shortest time to serve shall be styled the Chief Justice of Kentucky.

SEC. 7. If a vacancy shall occur in said Court, from any cause, the Governor shall issue a writ of election to the proper district to fill such vacancy for the residue of the term: *Provided*, That if the unexpired term be less than one year, the Governor shall appoint a Judge to fill such vacancy.

SEC. 8. No person shall be eligible to the office of Judge of the Court of Appeals who is not a citizen of the United States, a resident of the district for which he may be a candidate for two years next preceding his election, at least thirty years of age, and who has not been a practicing lawyer eight years, or whose service upon the bench of any court of record, when added to the time he may have practiced law, shall not be equal to eight years.

SEC. 9. The Court of Appeals shall hold its sessions at the seat of government, unless otherwise directed by law; but the General Assembly may, from time to time, direct that said

Court shall hold its sessions in any one or more of said districts.

SEC. 10. The first election of the Judges and Clerk or Clerks of the Court of Appeals shall take place on the second Monday in May 1851, and thereafter, in each district as a vacancy may occur, by the expiration of the term of office; and the Judges of the said Court shall be commissioned by the Governor.

SEC. 11. There shall be elected, by the qualified voters of this State, a Clerk of the Court of Appeals, who shall hold his office from the first election until the first Monday in August, 1858, and thereafter for the term or eight years from and after his election; and should the General Assembly provide for holding the Court of Appeals in any one or more of said districts, they shall also provide for the election of a Clerk by the qualified voters of such district, who shall hold his office for eight years, possess the same qualifications, and be subject to removal in the same manner as the Clerk of the Court of Appeals; but if the General Assembly shall, at its first or any other session, direct the Court of Appeals to hold its sessions in more than one district, a Clerk shall be elected by the qualified voters of such district. And the Clerk, first provided for in this section, shall be elected by the qualified voters of the district or districts. The same principle shall be observed whenever the Court shall be directed to hold its sessions in either of the other districts. Should the number of judges be reduced, the term of the office of Clerk shall be six years,

SEC. 12. No person shall be eligible to the office of Clerk of the Court of Appeals unless he be a citizen of the United States, a resident of the State two years next preceding his election, of the age of twenty-one years, and have a certificate from a Judge of the Court of Appeals, or a Judge of the Circuit Court, that he has been examined by the Clerk of his Court, under his supervision, and that he is qualified for the office for which he is a candidate.

SEC. 13. Should a vacancy occur in the office of Clerk of the Court of Appeals, the officer shall issue a writ of election, and the qualified voters of the State, or of the district in which the vacancy may occur, shall elect a Clerk of the Court of Appeals, to serve until the end of the term for which such Clerk was elected: *Provided*, That when a vacancy shall occur from any cause, or the Clerk be under charges upon information, the Judges of the Court of Appeals shall have power to appoint a Clerk *pro tem.*, to perform the duties of Clerk until such vacancy shall be filled, or the Clerk aquitted: *And provided further*, That no writ of election shall issue to fill a vacancy unless the unexpired term exceed one year.

SEC. 14. The General Assembly shall direct, by law, the the mode and manner of conducting and making due returns to the Secretary of of State, of all elections of the Judges and Clerk or Clerks of the Court of Appeals, and of determining contested elections of any of these officers.

SEC. 15. The General Assembly shall provide for an additional Judge or Judges, to constitute, with the remaining Judge or Judges, a special court for the trial of such cause or causes as may, at any time, be pending in the Court of Appeals, on the trial of which a majority of the Judges can not sit on account of interest in the event of the cause; or on account of their relationship to either party; or when a Judge may have been employed in or decided the cause in the inferior court.

Concerning the Circuit Courts.

SEC. 16. A Circuit Court shall be established in each county now existing, or which may hereafter be erected in this Commonwealth.

SEC. 17. The jurisdiction of said Court shall be and remain as now established, hereby giving to the General Assembly the power to change or alter it.

SEC. 18. The right to appeal or sue out a writ of error to the Court of Appeals shall remain as it now exists, until altered by law, hereby giving to the General Assembly the power to change, alter, or modify said right.

SEC. 19. At the first session after the adoption of this Constitution, the General Assembly shall divide the State into twelve judicial districts, having due regard to business, territory, and population: *Provided*, That no county shall be divided.

SEC. 20. They shall, at the same time that the judicial districts are laid off, direct elections to be held in each district, to elect a judge for said district, and shall prescribe in what manner the elections shall be conducted. The first election of Judges of the Circuit Courts shall take place on the second Monday in May, 1851; and afterwards on the first Monday in August, 1856, and on the first Monday in August in every sixth year thereafter.

SEC. 21. All persons qualified to vote for members of the General Assembly, in each district shall have the right to vote for Judges.

SEC. 22. No person shall be eligible as Judge of the Circuit Court who is not a citizen of the United States, a resident of the district for which he may be a candidate two years next preceding his election, at least thirty years of age, and who has not been a practicing lawyer eight years, or whose service upon the bench of any court of record, when added to the time he may have practiced law, shall not be equal to eight years.

SEC. 23. The Judges of the Circuit Court shall, after their first term, hold their office for the term of six years from the day of their election. They shall be commissioned by the Governor and continue in office until their successors be qualified, but shall be removable from office in the same manner as the Judges of the Court of Appeals; and the removal of a Judge from his district shall vacate his office.

SEC. 24. The General Assembly, if they deem it necessary, may establish one additional district every four years, but the judicial districts shall not exceed sixteen, until the population of this State shall exceed one million five hundred thousand.

SEC. 25. The Judges of the Circuit Court shall, at stated times, receive for their services an adequate compensation, to be fixed by law, which shall be equal and uniform throughout the State, and which shall not be diminished during the time for which they were elected.

SEC. 26. If a vacancy shall occur in the office of Judge of the Circuit Court, the Governor shall issue a writ of election to fill such vacancy for the residue of the term: *Provided*, That if the unexpired term be less than one year, the Governor shall appoint a Judge to fill such vacancy.

SEC. 27. The judicial districts of this State shall not be changed, except at the first session after an enumeration, unless when a new district may be established.

SEC. 28. The General Assembly shall provide by law for holding Circuit Courts, when, from any cause, the Judge shall fail to attend, or, if in attendance, can not properly preside.

Concerning County Courts.

SEC. 29. A County Court shall be established in each county now existing, or which may hereafter be erected within this Commonwealth, to consist of a Presiding Judge and two Associate Judges, any two of whom shall constitute a Court for the transaction of business: *Provided*, That the General Assembly may, at any time, abolish the office of the Associate Judges whenever it shall be deemed expedient; in which event they may associate with said Court any or all of the Justices of the Peace for the transaction of business.

SEC. 30. The Judges of the County Courts shall be elected by the qualified voters in each county for the term of four years, and shall continue in office until their successors be duly qualified, and shall receive such compensation for their services as may be provided for by law.

SEC. 31. The first election of County Court Judge shall

take place at the same time of the election of Judges of the Circuit Court, The Presiding Judge, first elected, shall hold his office until the first Monday in August, 1854. The Associate Judges shall hold their office until the first Monday in August, 1852, and until their successors be qualified ; and afterwards elections shall be held on the first Mondays in August, in the years in which vacancies regularly occur.

SEC. 32. No person shall be eligible to the office of Presiding or Associate Judge of the County Court, unless he be a citizen of the United States, over twenty-one years of age, and shall have been a resident of the county in which he shall be chosen one year next preceding the election.

SEC. 33. The jurisdiction of the County Court shall be regulated by law, and, until changed, shall be the same now vested in the County Courts of this State.

SEC. 34. Each county in this State shall be laid off into districts of convenient size, as the General Assembly may, from time to time, direct. Two Justices of the Peace shall be elected in each district. by the qualified voters therein, at such time and place as may be prescribed by law, for the term of four years, whose jurisdiction shall be co-extensive with the county ; no person shall be eligible as a Justice of the Peace unless he be a citizen of the United States, twenty-one years of age, and a resident of the district in which he may be a candidate.

SEC. 35. Judges of the County Court and Justices of the Peace shall be conservators of the peace. They shall be commissioned by the Governor. County and district officers shall vacate their offices by removal from the district or county in which they shall be appointed. The General Assembly shall provide, by law, the manner of conducting and making due returns of all elections of Judges of the County Court and Justices of the Peace, and for determining contested elections, and provide the mode of filling vacancies in these offices.

SEC. 36. Judges of the County Court and Justices of the

Peace, Sheriffs, Coroners, Surveyors, Jailers, County Assessors, Attorney for the County, and Constables, shall be subject to indictment or presentment for malfeasance or misfeasance in office, or willful neglect in the discharge of their official duties, in such mode as may be prescribed by law, subject to appeal to the Court of Appeals; and, upon conviction, their offices shall become vacant.

Sec. 37. The General Assembly may provide, by law, that the Justices of the Peace in each county shall sit at the Court of Claims and assist in laying the county levy and making appropriations only.

Sec. 38. When any city or town shall have a separate representation, such city or town, and the county in which it is located, may have such separate municipal courts, and executive and ministerial officers, as the General Assembly may, from time to time, provide.

Sec. 39. The Clerks of the Court of Appeals, Circuit and County Courts, shall be removable from office by the Court of Appeals, upon information and good cause shown. The Court shall be judges of the fact as well as the law. Two-thirds of the members present must concur in the sentence.

Sec 40. The Louisville Chancery Court shall exist, under this Constitution, subject to repeal, and its jurisdiction to enlargement and modification by the General Assembly. The Chancellor shall have the same qualifications as a Circuit Court Judge, and the Clerk of said Court as a Clerk of a Circuit Court, and the Marshal of said Court as a Sheriff, and the General Assembly shall provide for the election, by the qualified voters within its jurisdiction, of the Chancellor, Clerk, and Marshal of said Court, at the same time that the Judge and Clerk of the Circuit Court are elected for the county of Jefferson; and they shall hold their offices for the same time, and shall be removable in the same manner: *Provided*, That the Marshal of said court shall be ineligible for the succeeding term.

SEC. 41. The city court of Louisville, the Lexington city court, and all other police courts established in any city or town, shall remain, until otherwise directed by law, with their present powers and jurisdictions, and the judges, clerks, and marshals of such courts shall have the same qualifications, and shall be elected by the qualified voters of such cities or towns, at the same time and in the same manner, and hold their office for the same term as county judges, clerks, and sheriffs, respectively, and shall be liable to removal in the same manner. The General Assembly may vest judicial powers, for police purposes, in mayors of cities, police judges, and trustees of towns.

ARTICLE FIFTH,
Concerning Impeachments.

SEC. 1. The House of Representatives shall have the sole power of impeachment.

SEC. 2. All impeachments shall be tried by the Senate. When sitting for that purpose, the Senators shall be upon oath or affirmation No person shall be convicted without the concurrence of two-thirds of the members present.

SEC. 3. The Governor, and all civil officers, shall be liable to impeachment for any misdemeanor in office; but judgment in such cases shall not extend further than to removal from office, and disqualification to hold any office of honor, trust, or profit, under this Commonwealth; but the party convicted shall, nevertheless, be subject and liable to indictment, trial, and punishment by law.

ARTICLE SIXTH
Concerning Executive and Ministerial Offices for Counties and Districts.

SEC. 1. A Commonwealth's Attorney for each judicial district, and a circuit court clerk for each county shall be elected, whose term of office shall be the same as that of the circuit judges; also a county court clerk, an attorney, surveyor, coroner, and jailer, for each county, whose term of office shall be the same as that of the presiding judge of the county court.

Sec. 2. No person shall be eligible to the offices mentioned in this article who is not at the time twenty-four years old (except clerks of county and circuit courts, sheriffs, constables, and county attorneys, who shall be eligible at the age of twenty-one years), a citizen of the United States, and who has not resided two years, next preceding the election, in the State, and one year in the county or district for which he is a candidate. No person shall be eligibile to the office of Commonwealth's or county attorney unless he shall have been a licensed practicing attorney for two years. No person shall be eligible to the office of clerk, unless he shall have procured from a Judge of the Court of Appeals, or a judge of the circuit court, a certificate that he has been examined by the clerk of his court under his supervision, and that he is qualified for the office for which he is a candidate.

Sec. 3. The Commonwealth's Attorney and circuit court clerk shall be elected at the same time as the circuit judge—the Commonwealth's Attorney by the qualified voters of the district, the circuit court clerk by the qualified voters of the county. The county attorney, clerk, surveyor, coroner, and jailer, shall be elected at the same time, and in the same manner, as the presiding judge of the county court.

Sec. 4. A sheriff shall be elected in each county, by the qualified voters thereof, whose term of office shall, after the first term, be two years, and until his successor be qualified; and he shall be re-eligible for a second term; but no sheriff shall, after the expiration of the second term be re-eligible, or act as deputy, for the succeeding term. The first election of sheriffs shall be on the second Monday in May, 1851; and the sheriffs then elected shall hold their offices until the first Monday in January, 1853, and until their successors be qualified; and on the first Monday in August, 1852, and on the first Monday of August in every second year thereafter, elections for sheriff shall be held: *Provided*, That the sheriffs first elected shall enter upon the duties of their respective offices on the first Monday in June, 1851, and, after the first election, on the first Monday in January next succeeding their election.

SEC. 5. A constable shall be elected in every justices' district, who shall be chosen for two years, at such time and place as may be provided by law, whose jurisdiction shall be co-extensive with the county in which he may reside.

SEC. 6. Officers for towns and cities shall be elected for such terms, and in such manner, and with such qualifications as may be prescribed by law.

SEC. 7. Vacancies in offices under this article shall be filled until the next regular election, in such manner as the General Assembly may provide.

SEC. 8. When a new county shall be erected, officers for the same, to serve until the next stated election, shall be elected or appointed in such way and at such times as the General Assembly may prescribe.

SEC. 9. Clerks, sheriffs, surveyors, coroners, constables, and jailers, and such other officers, as the General Assembly may, from time to time, require, shall, before they enter upon the duties of their respective offices, and as often thereafter as may be deemed proper, give such bond and security as shall be prescribed by law.

SEC. 10. The General Assembly may provide for the election or appointment, for a term not exceeding four years, of such other county or district ministerial and executive officers, as shall, from time to time, be necessary and proper.

SEC. 11. A county assessor shall be elected in each county at the same time, and for the same term, that the presiding judge of the county court is elected, until otherwise provided for by law. He shall have power to appoint such assistants as may be necessary and proper.

ARTICLE SEVENTH.
Concerning the Militia.

Sec. 1. The militia of this Commonwealth shall consist of all free, able-bodied male persons (negroes, mulattoes, and Indians excepted) resident in the same, between the ages of eighteen and forty-five years, except such persons as now are, or hereafter may be, exempted by the laws of the United States, or of this State; but those who belong to religious societies whose tenets forbid them to carry arms, shall not be compelled to do so, but shall pay an equivalent for personal services.

Sec. 2. The Governor shall appoint the Adjutant General and his other staff officers; the Major Generals, Brigadier Generals, and Commandants of Regiments shall, respectively, appoint their staff officers; and commandants of companies shall appoint their non-commissioned officers.

Sec. 3. All militia officers, whose appointment is not herein otherwise provided for, shall be elected by persons subject to military duty within their respective companies, battalions, regiments, brigades and divisions, under such rules and regulations, and for such terms, not exceeding six years, as the General Assembly may, from time to time, direct and establish.

ARTICLE EIGHTH.
General Provisions.

Sec. 1. Members of the General Assembly, and all officers, before they enter upon the execution of the duties of their respective offices, and all members of the bar, before they enter upon the practice of their profession, shall take the following oath or affirmation : I do solemnly swear (or affirm, as the case may be) that I will support the Constitution of the United States and the Constitution of this State, and be faithful and true to the Commonwealth of Kentucky, so long as I continue a citizen thereof, and that I will faithfully execute, to the best of my abilities, the office of ———— ————, according to law; and I do further solemnly swear (or affirm) that since the adoption of the present Constitution, I, being a citizen of this State, have not fought a duel with deadly weapons within this State, nor out of it, with a citizen of this State, nor have I sent or accepted a challenge to fight a duel with deadly weapons with a citizen of this State; nor have I acted as second in carrying a challenge, or aided or assisted any person thus offending—so help me God.

SEC. 2. Treason against the Commonwealth shall consist only in levying war against it, or in adhering to its enemies, giving them aid and comfort. No person shall be convicted of treason, unless on the testimony of two witnesses to the same overt act, or his own confession in open court.

SEC. 3. Every person shall be disqualified from holding any office of trust or profit for the term for which he shall have been elected, who shall be convicted of having given or offered any bribe or treat to procure his election.

SEC. 4. Laws shall be made to exclude from office and from suffrage those who shall thereafter be convicted of bribery, perjury, forgery, or other crimes or high misdemeanors. The privilege of free suffrage shall be supported by laws regulating elections, and prohibiting, under adequate penalties, all undue influence thereon from power, bribery, tumult, or other improper practices.

SEC. 5. No money shall be drawn from the Treasury but in pursuance of appropriations made by law, nor shall any appropriations of money for the support of an army be made for a longer time than two years; and a regular statement and account of the receipts and expenditures of all public money shall be published annually.

SEC. 6. The General Assembly may direct, by law, in what manner, and in what courts, suits may be brought against the Commonwealth.

SEC. 7. The manner of administering an oath or affirmation shall be such as is most consistent with the conscience of the deponent, and shall be esteemed by the General Assembly the most solemn appeal to God.

SEC. 8. All laws which, on the first day of June, one thousand seven hundred and ninety-two, were in force in the State of Virginia, and which are of a general nature, and not local to that State, and not repugnant to this Constitution, nor to the laws which have been enacted by the General Assembly of this Commonwealth, shall be in force within this State until they shall be altered or repealed by the General Assembly.

SEC. 9. The compact with the State of Virginia, subject to such alterations as may be made therein agreeably to the mode prescribed to by the said compact, shall be considered as part of the Constitution.

SEC. 10. It shall be the duty of the General Assembly to pass such laws as shall be necessary and proper to decide differences by arbitrators, to be appointed by the parties who may choose that summary mode of adjustment.

SEC. 11. All civil officers for the Commonwealth at large shall reside within the State, and all district. county, or town officers, within their respective districts, counties or towns (trustees of towns excepted), and shall keep their offices at such places therein as may be required by law; and all militia officers shall reside in the bounds of the division, brigade, regiment, battalion, or company to which they may severally belong.

SEC. 12. Absence on the business of this State, or the United States, shall not forfeit a residence once obtained, so as to deprive any one of the right of suffrage, or of being elected or appointed to any office under this Commonwealth, under the exceptions contained in this Constitution.

SEC. 13. It shall be the duty of the General Assembly to regulate, by law, in what cases, and what deductions from the salaries of public officers shall be made for neglect of duty in their official capacity.

SEC. 14. Returns of all elections by the people shall be made to the Secretary of State, for the time being, except in those cases otherwise provided for in this Constitution, or which shall be otherwise directed by law.

SEC. 15. In all elections by the people, and also by the Senate and House of Representatives, jointly or separately, the votes shall be personally and publicly given *viva voce:* *Provided*, That dumb persons entitled to suffrage, may vote by ballot.

SEC. 16. All elections by the people shall be held between the hours of six o'clock in the morning and seven o'clock in the evening.

SEC. 17. The General Assembly shall, by law, prescribe the time when the several officers authorized or directed by this Constitution to be elected or appointed shall enter upon the duties of their respective offices, except where the time is fixed by this Constitution.

SEC. 18. No member of Congress, no person holding or exercising any office of trust or profit under the United States, or either of them, or under any foreign power, shall be eligible as a member of the General Assembly of this Commonwealth, or hold or exercise any office of trust or profit under the same.

SEC. 19. The General Assembly shall direct, by law, how persons who now are, or may hereafter become, securities for public officers, may be relieved or discharged on account of such securityship.

SEC. 20. Any person who shall, after the adoption of this Constitution, either directly or indirectly, give, accept, or knowingly carry a challenge to any person or persons, to fight in single combat, with a citizen of this State, with any deadly weapon, either in or out of the State, shall be deprived of the right to hold any office of honor or profit in this Commonwealth, and shall be punished otherwise in such manner as the General Assembly may prescribe by law.

Sec. 21. The Governor shall have power, after five years from the time of the offense, to pardon all persons who shall have in anywise participated in a duel, either as principals, seconds, or otherwise, and to restore him or them to all the rights, privileges, and immunities to which he or they are entitled before such participation. And upon the presentation of such pardon, the oath prescribed in the first section of this article shall be varied to suit the case.

Sec. 22. At its first session after the adoption of this Constitution, the General Assembly shall appoint not more than three persons, learned in the law, whose duty it shall be to revise and arrange the statute laws of this Commonwealth, both civil and criminal, so as to have but one law on any one subject; and also three other persons, learned in the law, whose duty it shall be to prepare a code of practice for the courts, both civil and criminal, in this Commonwealth, by abridging and simplifying the rules of practice and laws in relation thereto; all of whom shall, at as early a day as practicable, report the result of their labors to the General Assembly, for their adoption or modification.

Sec. 23. So long as the Board of Internal Improvement shall be continued, the president thereof shall be elected by the qualified voters of this Commonwealth, and hold the office for the term of four years, and until another be duly elected and qualified. The election shall be held at the same time, and be conducted in the same manner, as the election for Governor of this Commonwealth under this Constitution; but nothing herein contained shall prevent the General Assembly from abolishing said Board of Internal Improvement, or the office of president thereof.

Sec. 24. The General Assembly shall provide, by law, for the trial of any contested election of Auditor, Register, Treasurer, Attorney Generals, Judges of Circuit Courts, and all other officers not otherwise herein specified.

SEC. 25. The General Assembly shall provide, by law, for the making of the returns, by the proper officers, of the election of all officers to be elected under this Constitution; and the Governor shall issue commissions to the Auditor, Register, Treasurer, President of the Board of Internal Improvement, Superintendent of Public Instruction, and such other officers as he may be directed by law to commission, as soon as he has ascertained the result of the election of those officers respectively.

SEC. 26. When a vacancy shall happen in the office of Attorney General, Auditor of Public Accounts, Treasurer, Register of the Land Office, President of the Board of Internal Improvement, or Superintendent of Public Instruction, the Governor, in the recess of the Senate, shall have power to fill the vacancy by granting commissions which shall expire at the end of the next session, and shall fill the vacancy for the balance of the time by and with the advice and consent of the Senate.

ARTICLE NINTH.
Concerning the Seat of Government.

The seat of government shall continue in the city of Frankfort, until it shall be removed by law; *Provided, however,* That two-thirds of the members elected to each house of the General Assembly shall concur in the passage of such law.

ARTICLE TENTH.
Concerning Slaves.

SEC. 1. The General Assembly shall have no power to pass laws for the emancipation of slaves, without the consent of their owners, or without paying their owners previous to such emancipation, a full equivalent in money for the slaves so emancipated, and providing for their removal from the State.

They shall have no power to prevent emigrants to this State from bringing with them such persons as are deemed slaves by the laws of any of the United States, so long as any person of the same age or description shall be continued in slavery by the laws of this State. They shall pass laws to permit owners of slaves to emancipate them, saving the rights of creditors, and to prevent them from remaining in this State after they are emancipated. They shall have full power to prevent slaves being brought into this State, who have been, since the first of January, one thousand seven hundred and eighty-nine, or may hereafter be imported into any of the United States from a foreign country. And they shall have full power to pass such laws as may be necessary to oblige the owners of slaves to treat them with humanity; to provide for them necessary clothing and provision; to abstain from all injuries to them, extending to life or limb; and in case of their neglect or refusal to comply with the directions of such laws, to have such slave or slaves sold for the benefit of the owner or owners.

SEC. 2. The General Assembly shall pass laws, providing that any free negro or mulatto hereafter emigrating to, and any slave hereafter emancipated in, and refusing to leave this State, or having left it, shall return and settle within this State, shall be deemed guilty of felony, and punished by confinement in the penitentiary thereof.

SEC. 3. In the prosecution of slaves for felony, no inquest by a grand jury shall be necessary; but the proceedings in such prosecution shall be regulated by law, except that the General Assembly shall have no power to deprive them of the privilege of an impartial trial by petit jury.

ARTICLE ELEVENTH.

Concerning Education.

SEC. 1, The capital of the fund called and known as the "Common School Fund," consisting of one million two hundred and twenty-five thousand seven hundred and sixty-eight dollars and forty-two cents, for which bonds have been executed by the State to the Board of Education, and seventy-three thousand five hundred dollars of stock in the Bank of Kentucky; also the sum of fifty-one thousand two hundred and twenty-three dollars and twenty-nine cents, balance of interest on the school fund for the year 1848, unexpended, together with any sum which may be hereafter raised in the State, by taxation or otherwise, for purposes of education, shall be held inviolate, for the purpose of sustaining a system of common schools· The interest and dividends of said funds, together with any sum which may be produced for that purpose, by taxation or otherwise, may be appropriated in aid of common schools, but for no other purpose. The General Assembly shall invest said fifty-one thousand two hundred and twenty-three dollars and twenty-nine cents in some safe and profitable manner; and any portion of the interest and dividends of said school fund, or other money or property raised for school purposes, which may not be needed in sustaining common schools, shall be vested in like manner. The General Assembly shall make provision, by law, for the payment of the interest of said fund: *Provided*, That each county shall be entitled to its portion of the income of said fund; and if not called for common school purposes, it shall be reinvested, from time to time, for the benefit of said county.

SEC. 2. A Superintendent of Public Instruction shall be elected by the qualified voters of this Commonwealth, at the same time the Governor is elected, who shall hold his office for four years, and his duties and salary shall be prescribed and fixed by law.

ARTICLE TWELFTH.

Mode of Revising the Constitution.

SEC. 1. When experience shall point out the necessity of amending this Constitution, and when a majority of all the members elected to each house of the General Assembly shall, within the first twenty days of any regular session, concur in passing a law for taking the sense of the good people of this Commonwealth as to the necessity and expediency of calling a convention, it shall be the duty of the several sheriffs, and other officers of election, at the next general election which shall be held for Representatives to the General Assembly, after the passage of such law, to open a poll for and make return to the Secretary of State, for the time being, of the names of all those entitled to vote for Representative, who have voted for calling a convention; and if, thereupon, it shall appear that a majority of all the citizens of the State, entitled to vote for Representatives, have voted for calling a convention, the General Assembly shall, at their next regular session, direct that a similar poll shall be opened and return made for the next election for Representatives ; and if, thereupon, it shall appear that a majority of all the citizens of the State entitled to vote for Representatives have voted for calling a convention, the General Assembly shall, at their next session, pass a law calling a convention, to consist of as many members as there shall be in the House of Representatives, and no more; to be chosen on the first Monday in August thereafter, in the same manner and proportion, and at the same places, and possessed of the same qualifications as of a qualified elector, by citizens entitled to vote for Representatives; and to meet within three months after their election, for the purpose of re-adopting, amending, or changing this Constitution; but if it shall appear by the vote of either year, as aforesaid, that a majority of all the citizens entitled to vote for Representatives, did not vote for calling a convention, a convention shall not then be called. And for the purpose of ascertaining whether a majority of the citizens, entitled to vote for Representatives, did or did not vote for calling a convention as above, the General Assembly passing the law authorizing such vote shall provide for ascertaing the number of citizens entitled to vote for Representatives within the State.

Sec. 2. The convention, when assembled, shall judge of the election of its members and decide contested elections; but the General Assembly shall, in calling a convention, provide for taking testimony in such cases, and for issuing a writ of election in case of a tie.

ARTICLE THIRTEENTH.

Bill of Rights.

That the general, great, and essential principles of liberty and free government may be recognized and established WE DECLARE—

Sec. 1. That all freemen, when they form a social compact, are equal, and that no man, or set of men, are entitled to exclusive, separate public emoluments or privileges from the community, but in consideration of public services.

Sec. 2. The absolute, arbitrary power over the lives, liberty, and property of freemen exists nowhere in a republic— not even in the largest majority.

Sec. 3. The right of property is before and higher than any constitutional sanction; and the right of the owner of a slave to such slave, and its increase, is the same, and as inviolable as the right of the owner of any property whatever.

Sec. 4. That all power is inherent in the people, and all free governments are founded on their authority, and instituted for their peace, safety, happiness, security, and the protection of property. For the advancement of these ends, they have at all times an inalienable and indefeasable right to alter, reform, or abolish their government, in such manner as they may think proper.

Sec. 5. That all men have a natural and indefeasable right to worship Almighty God according to the dictates of their own consciences; that no man shall be compelled to attend, erect, or support any place of worship, or to maintain any ministry against his consent; that no human authority ought, in any case whatever, to control or interfere with the rights of conscience; and that no preference shall be given, by law, to any religious societies or modes of worship.

Sec. 6. That the civil rights, privileges, or capacities of any citizen shall in nowise be diminished or enlarged on account of his religion.

Sec. 7. That all elections shall be free and equal.

Sec. 8. That the ancient mode of trial by jury shall be held sacred, and the right thereof remain inviolate, subject to such modifications as may be authorized by this Constitution.

Sec. 9. That printing presses shall be free to every person who undertakes to examine the proceedings of the General Assembly, or any branch of government, and no law shall ever be made to restrain the right thereof. The free communication of thoughts and opinions is one of the invaluable rights of man, and every citizen may freely speak, write, and print on any subject, being responsible for the abuse of that liberty.

Sec. 10. In prosecutions for the publication of papers investigating the official conduct of officers or men in a public capacity, or where the matter published is proper for public information, the truth thereof may be given in evidence; and in all indictments for libels, the jury shall have a right to determine the law and the facts, under the direction of the court, as in other cases.

Sec. 11. That the people shall be secure in their persons, houses, papers, and possessions, from unreasonable seizures and searches, and that no warrant to search any place or to seize any person or thing, shall issue, without describing them as nearly as may be, nor without probable cause, supported by oath or affirmation.

Sec. 12. That in all criminal prosecutions, the accused hath a right to be heard by himself and counsel; to demand the nature and cause of the accusation against him; to meet the witnesses face to face; to have compulsory process for obtaining witnesses in his favor; and in prosecutions by indictment or information, a speedy public trial by an impartial jury of the vicinage; that he can not be compelled to give evidence against himself; nor can he be deprived of his life, liberty, or property, unless by the judgment of his peers or the law of the land.

SEC. 13. That no person shall, for any indictable offense, be proceeded against criminally, by information, except in cases arising in the land or naval forces, or in the militia when in actual service, in time of war or public danger, or by leave of the court, for oppression or misdemeanor in office.

SEC. 14. No person shall, for the same offense, be twice put in jeopardy of his life or limb; nor shall any man's property be taken or applied to public use, without the consent of his representatives, and without just compensation being previously made to him.

SEC. 15. That all courts shall be open, and every person, for an injury done him in his lands, goods, person, or reputation, shall have remedy by the due course of law, and right and justice administered, without sale, denial, or delay.

SEC. 16. That no power of suspending laws shall be exercised, unless by the General Assembly, or its authority.

SEC. 17. That excessive bail shall not be required, nor excessive fines imposed, nor cruel punishments inflicted.

SEC. 18. That all prisoners shall be bailable by sufficient securities, unless for capital offenses, when the proof is evident or presumption great; and the privilege of the writ of *habeas corpus* shall not be suspended, unless when, in cases of rebellion or invasion, the public safety may require it.

SEC. 19. That the person of a debtor, where there is not strong presumption of fraud, shall not be continued in prison after delivering up his estate for the benefit of his creditors, in such manner as shall be prescribed by law.

SEC. 20. That no *ex post facto* law; nor any law impairing contracts, shall be made.

SEC. 21. That no person shall be attainted of treason or felony by the General Assembly.

SEC. 22. That no attainder shall work corruption of blood, nor, except during the life of the offender, forfeiture of estate to the Commonwealth.

SEC. 23. That the estates of such persons as shall destroy their own lives, shall descend or vest as in case of natural death; and if any person shall be killed by casualty, there shall be no forfeiture by reason thereof.

SEC. 24. That the citizens have a right, in a peaceable manner, to assemble together for their common good, and to apply to those invested with the powers of government for redress of grievances or other proper purposes, by petition, address, or remonstrance.

SEC. 25. That the rights of the citizens to bear arms in defense of themselves and the State shall not be questioned, but the General Assembly may pass laws to prevent persons from carrying concealed arms.

SEC. 26. That no standing army shall, in time of peace, be kept up without the consent of the General Assembly; and the military shall, in all cases, and at all times, be in strict subordination to the civil power.

SEC. 27. That no soldier shall, in time of peace, be quartered in any house without the consent of the owner; nor in time of war, but in a manner to be prescribed by law.

SEC. 28. That the General Assembly shall not grant any title of nobility, or hereditary distinction, nor create any office the appointment to which shall be for a longer time than for a term of years.

SEC. 29. That immigration from the State shall not be prohibited.

SEC. 30. To guard against transgressions of the high powers which we have delegated, WE DECLARE, that everything in this article is excepted out of the general powers of government, and shall forever remain inviolate; and that all laws contrary thereto, or contrary to this Constitution shall be void.

SCHEDULE.

That no inconvenience may arise from the alterations and amendments made in the Constitution of this Commonwealth, and in order to carry the same into complete operation, it is hereby declared and ordained:

SEC. 1. That all the laws of this Commonwealth in force at the time of the adoption of this Constitution, and not inconsistent therewith, and all rights, actions, prosecutions, claims, and contracts, as well of individuals as of bodies corporate, shall continue as if this Constitution had not been adopted.

SEC. 2. The oaths of office herein directed to be taken may be administered by any judge or justice of the peace, until the General Assembly shall otherwise direct.

SEC. 3. No office shall be superseded by the adoption of this Constitution; but the laws of the State relative to the duties of the several officers, Legislative, Executive, Judicial, and Military, shall remain in full force, though the same be contrary to this Constitution, and the several duties shall be performed by the respective officers of the State, according to the existing laws, until the organization of the Government, as provided for under this Constitution, and the entering into office of the officers to be elected or appointed under said government, and no longer.

SEC. 4. It shall be the duty of the General Assembly which shall convene in the year 1850, to make an apportionment of the representation of this State, upon the principles set forth in this Constitution; and until the first apportionment shall be made as herein directed, the apportionment of Senators and Representatives among the several districts and counties in this State shall remain as at present fixed by law: *Provided*, That on the first Monday in August, 1850, all Senators shall go out of office, and on that day an election for Senators and

Representatives shall be held throughout the State, and those then elected shall hold their offices for one year, and no longer: *Provided further*, That at the elections to be held in the year 1850, that provision in this Constitution which requires voters to vote in the precinct within which they reside, shall not apply.

Sec. 5. All recognizances heretofore taken, or which may be taken before the organization of the judicial department under this Constitution, shall remain as valid as though this Constitution had not been adopted, and may be prosecuted in the name of the Commonwealth. All criminal prosecutions and penal actions, which have arisen, or may arise before the reorganization of the judicial department under this Constitution, may be prosecuted to judgment and execution, in the name of the Commonwealth.

"We, the representatives of the freemen of Kentucky, in convention assembled, in their name, and by the authority of the Commonwealth of Kentucky, and in virtue of the powers, vested in us, as delegates from the counties respectively affixed to our names, do ordain and proclaim the foregoing to be the Constitution of the Commonwealth of Kentucky, from and after this day.

"Done at Frankfort, this eleventh day of June, in the year of our Lord one thousand eight hundred and fifty, and in the fifty-ninth year of the Commonwealth.

JAMES GUTHRIE.
President of the Convention, and Member from the City of Louisville.

Attest
THO. J. HELM,
Secretary of the Convention.

THO. D. TILFORD.
Assistant Secretary.

Index.

PART FIRST.

A

Abolition of Slavery	23
Adams Jno.	15-17
Adams Sam'l	16
Albemarle Colony	13
Amendments to Constitution	23
How made	24-46
American Association	16
Andros Gov	12
Aristocratic Government	6
ARTICLES OF CONFEDERATION	95
Digest of	16, 17, 18
Defects of	18
Revision proposed	20
Nature of	18

B

Boston Port Bill	15
Boston Tea Party	15
Burr and Jefferson	23

C

Carteret Colony	31
Charter Government	8
Charter Oak	12
Civil Laws	6
Colonial Meetings	15
Committee of States	19
Connecticut	12
Constitution Def	6
Constitution signed	21
Convention to Revise Art. of Con.	20

D

DECLARATION OF INDEPENDENCE	89
Formation of	17
Declaration Col. Rights	7
Delaware	13
Democratic Government	6
Discovery of America	8

F

First Constitution	18
First Continental Congress	15
First Inauguration	22
First Legal Declaration of Liberty of Conscience	13
First Legislative Body in America	9
First President, Election of	22
First *Written* Constitution	12
Forms of Government	5
Fourth of March	22
Franklin Benj	17-21

G

Georgia	14
Germs of Liberty	5

H

Habeas Corpus Act	7
Hamilton Alex	21
Henry Patrick	16

I

Independence Advocated	17

J

Jay Jno 16
Jefferson Thomas 17

L

Lee Richard Henry 1
Lexington 16
Livingston Robert R 17
Lord Baltimore 11

M

Madison Jas. 21
Madison Papers 21
Magna Charta 6
Maryland 11
Massachusetts 10
Mayflower 10
Military Laws 6
Monarchical Government 5
Morris Robt 21
Mutiny Act 15

N

Navigation Act 11
New Hampshire 11
New Jersey 13
New York 10
North Carolina 13

O

Oglethorpe Jas 14
Oxford College 7

P

Parliament 7
Parliamentary Laws 6
Patriarchal Government 5
Penn Wm 14
Pennsylvania 14
President—Consti. Conv. 21
Proprietary Government 9

R

Randolph Peyton 15-16
Ratification Art. of Con. 18
Ratification Constitution 21

Republican Government 6
Revolution, Causes of 14
Rhode Island 9-12

S

Second Continental Congress . . . 16
Sherman Roger 16-17
South Carolina 13
Stamp Act 15
States' Rights 18
Suffrage 29
Sugar Act 15
Swedes 13

T

Taxes 18
Tax on Tea 15
Theocratic Government 5
Toleration Act 11
Treaty of Peace 16
Trial by Jury 7

U

United Colonies New England . . 10

V

Virginia 9
Voting 19

W

Washington George 15-21
Williams Roger 21

PART SECOND.

A

Apportionment, Table of 31
Area, U. S. 25
Army and Navy 44
Attainder, Bill of 45
Attorney General 70
   His duties, etc 70-71
Appointing power of President . . 54
Army Officers, Rank and Pay . . . 62

INDEX.

B

Bank Notes 59
Beck Jas. B. 27
Benton Thos. H. 28
Bill 37
   How introduced 37
   How it becomes a law 37-38
   Leave 37
   Leave Days 37
   Readings of bill 37
   Signatures bill must have . . . 38
Blackburn, J. C. S. 27
Borrowing Money 43
Branches of Government 26

C

Cabinet 54
Census 29-66
Coining money 43
Commander-in-chief 61
Committee on Ways and Means . . 36
Committees of Senate 87
Committees of House 88
Comparative Governments . . . 84-85
Congress 27
   Length of Term 27
   Longest term 27
   Powers of 42
   Powers denied 45-46
Congressmen 33
   Eligibility 28
   How elected, term, salary, mileage, vacancy, etc 33
Constitution of U. S. 106-126
Copyright 44
Cost of European Sovereigns . . . 48
Courts of U. S. 73
   Diagram of same 73-74
   Officers 74 75
   Supreme Court 44 73
   Circuit Courts 77 78
   Court of Claims 80
   District Courts 79 80
   Court of District of Columbia . . 81
   Territorial Courts 81

D

Dead Letters 68 69
Declaration of Independence . . 89-94
Department of Agriculture 71
Department of Justice 71
Department of State 55
District of Columbia 44 45

E

Elections 49-51
Election of U. S. Senator 32
Electoral College 50
   Meeting of 51
Electoral Commission 41
Election by Popular Vcte 52 53
Election by House of Rep 52
Enacting Clause 39
Exclusive Powers of Senate 39
Exclusive Powers of House 40
Executive Department 46
   President 46
   Character of 46
   Eligibility 47
   Salary 47
   How paid 48
   Term of office 48
   Powers and duties 72
Executive Sessions 39
Expost-facto Law 45

F

Fiscal Year 71
Foreign Ministers 57
Franking Privilege 33

H

Hays R. B. 41
House of Representatives 28
   Organization of 35
   Speaker of 35
   Other officers and their duties . . 36

I

Impeachment 40 41
Inauguration 53

Interior Department 64
   Bureaus of 64 65
Internal Revenue 45

J

Johnson R. M. 39
Judicial Department 72
Juries 81

K

Kinds of Liberty 25

L

Legislation 37
Legislative Department 26

M

Meeting of Congress 33
Military Academy 62
Motto of United States 25

N

Naturalization Laws 43
Navy Department 63
Naval Officers, Rank and Pay of . 64

O

Oath of Office 53

P

Patriarchal Goverment 5
Presidential Directory 85
President's Message 36
Presidential Succession Bill . . . 49
Population of U S. (table) 83
Post Office Department . . . 67
Postage, Rates of 69
Post Master General 67
   His duties 68
Proroguing 42
Prosperity of U. S 25
Public Debt 61
Public Grounds 45

R

Relative Powers and Duties of
   Senate and House of Rep . . 38 39
Revenue 60 61

S

Secretary of State 55
Secretary of Treasury 59
Senate, How composed 27
   Length of term 27
   Organization of 33
   Officers of 34
   Rules of Senate and House . . . 35

T

Tariff 42
Taxes 42
Treasury Department 59
Treaties 40

V

Vice-President 48
   Duty 48
   Rank 48
   Power in Senate 48
Voting in Congress 41

W

War Department 61
War Footing of United States . . . 61

PART THIRD.

A

Adjutant General 153
Apportionments 140
Arson 178
Assessor 174
Attorney General 156
Attorney, Commonwealth's 163
Attorney County 169
Auditor 155
   His report 156

B

Bill of Rights 149
Board of Equalization 158
Board of Supervisors 174
Burglary 178

INDEX.

C

City Government	183
Clerk of Appellate Courts	160
Clerk of Circuit Courts	162
Clerk of County Courts	169
Commissioner of Agriculture	153
Commissioner of Mines	154
Compact with Virginia	132
Constable	172
Constitution, First	133
Constitution, Second	136
Constitution, Present	139
Constitution of Kentucky	191
Coroner	176
Counterfeiting	179
County Surveyor	179
Courts, Kinds of	159
Court of Appeals	160
Superior Court	162
Circuit Courts	162
County Courts	167
Quarterly Courts	170
Magisterial Courts	171
Franklin Circuit Court	170
Crimes and Punishments	177

D

Districts—	
Appellate	187
Circuit Court	188
Congressional	190
Senatorial	186

E

Elections and Returns	179
Embezzlement	179
Executive Department	149

F

Felony	177
Forgery	179

G

Governor	149

H

House of Representatives	140–143

J

Jailer	175
Judges—	
Appellate	160
Superior Court	162
Circuit	163
County	167
Judicial Department	159
Juries	164

K

Kentucky	129
Kentucky District	132
Kentucky, Separation from Va.	132

L

Larceny	178
Law, First enacted	134
Legislation	146
Legislative Department	140
Legislature First	134
Legislature, Organization of	143
Lieutenant Governor	150
Local Government	127

M

Maiming	178
Manslaughter	177
Misdemeanor	177
Municipal Government	183
Murder	177

P

Part Third	127
Perjury	178
Public Printer	159

R

Register Land Office	157
Robbery	177

S

Secretary of State	152
Senate	141

INDEX.

Shelby Isaac 134
Sheriff 173
State Geologist 153
State Librarian 159
Supt. Public Schools 175
Supt. Public Instruction . . 151

T

Treason 177
Treasurer 154

www.ingramcontent.com/pod-product-compliance
Lightning Source LLC
Chambersburg PA
CBHW021807230426
43669CB00008B/659